Building Self-Esteem
in Children

Building Self-Esteem in Children

Patricia H. Berne and Louis M. Savary

CONTINUUM · NEW YORK

1993
The Continuum Publishing Company
370 Lexington Avenue, New York, N.Y. 10017

Printed in the United States of America

Library of Congress Cataloging in Publication Data
Berne, Patricia H.
   Building self-esteem in children.
   1. Child psychology. 2. Self-respect. 3. Children—
Management. I. Savary, Louis M. II. Title.
HQ769.B5214   649'.1   81-3237   ISBN 0-8264-0050-7   AACR2
ISBN 0-8264-0353-0 (pbk.)

Contents

III ★ Nurturing Success   46

IV ★ Bridging to a Loving World   77

Authors' Note

Working alongside Mrs. Gladys Chilton, my first mentor as a primary school teacher, I watched the incredibly effective way she had of teaching children. With her expert touch, learning even academic skills was exciting and fun. Children in her class always felt valued by her and good about themselves. She said many people had asked her to write her classroom techniques in a book, but because she was so busy teaching she never got around to it. As far as I know, she never did. During that year with her, I thought maybe someday I'd write what I could remember of them for her.

Years later, when in my master's thesis I presented a procedure I called tutoring-therapy, people who read it said they wished I would write a manual of techniques so that others could use them. I thought maybe someday I'd also write that manual.

This book is an attempt to fulfill a part of both these wishes. I want to share not only techniques, but also underlying principles that influence self-esteem in children. Nurturing self-esteem in children, building in opportunities for success, facilitating a positive self-image are all important influences on a child's healthy development. My intent is to help adults be conscious of the power of these influences on children and to use them in constructive ways to promote healthy growth.

Like Mrs. Chilton, I resist the discipline of writing out my thoughts, even though I know and have been told they would be useful. For whatever did get written, I have my partner and coauthor Louis M. Savary to thank. It was his interest and energy that drew much of this information out of me and shaped it into a manuscript. So, while the personal experiences in these pages are mostly mine (Berne), the underlying principles of self-esteem are clearly his as well as mine, part of his life as well as mine. (To protect confidentiality, the names of all children have been changed as well as other details that might reveal their personal identity.)

From our professional work and our experience with children, we have been noting simple ways for creating a loving climate and developing healthy self-esteem. We showed these notes to friends and colleagues in the helping professions, who told us we had formulated the essence of what goes on in much effective therapy and in the therapeutic relationships, as well as in loving relationships generally. This book contains essentially the collection of ideas in those notes.

It is not meant to substitute for professional psychotherapy when such therapy is appropriate. However, in many cases, concerned friends and family of a child with emotional problems and low self-esteem often wonder, "What can *we* do to help?" The principles offered here provide a kind of complement to many forms of professional therapy; they have been used successfully with many children. I've used them, first, as a mother with my three stepchildren and my own three daughters, from early childhood through high school; next, as a teacher, tutor, and therapist with children, handicapped and normal, in nursery and elementary schools; and then, as a counselor with young people in high school and college.

We share these suggestions and principles with you in the hope you will make them a part of your relationships with children. We hope you will use them consciously, and in your loving effort to foster self-esteem in children you will experience yourself as a caring person. Through these suggestions we hope you will find ways to express what is in your heart and to be the true friend you want to be to children.

As you touch a child's life with your caring and valuing, you will feel that same touch upon your own life. When you are valuing a child, you also experience yourself as more valuable and lovable.

In this spirit, then, we share these ideas and principles with you, along with our own personal wishes for the enrichment of your relationships with children and our hope that you may know the joy of living with children in a climate of love and mutual self-esteem.

Patricia H. Berne
Louis M. Savary

Creating an Atmosphere Where Self-Esteem Can Grow

In childhood my self-esteem was not nurtured, and I came to believe many negative things about myself. As I got older, the power of my negative self-image grew harder to deal with since its roots had been planted early. Although many events in my life today attempt to promote healthy self-esteem in me, the devalued and disapproved child that continues to live inside me still insists on putting me down.

Therefore, it is not surprising that for years my work has focused upon the self-esteem needs of children. My hope has been to find ways of reversing a child's budding negative self-image at its early stages. This is the basic thrust of the procedure I devised which I named tutoring-therapy. With my skills in tutoring, I could facilitate built-in success in a child's academic life, and with my knowledge of psychology I could work for success in ego growth and interpersonal relationships. I found there was potential for a therapeutic relationship in almost every tutoring situation; together, tutoring and therapy could be used to help reverse a child's negative self-image by working toward a positive one, and to reverse a failure cycle by working toward a sense of competence, success, and value.

I remember talking with a woman friend of mine, Sally, the mother of five children. One day as we sat together on the beach and watched our children play, Sally told me she had a very wise uncle. She thought he was very wise because she felt he had given her the most important piece of wisdom about raising children anyone ever had. Naturally, I asked her what that wisdom was. She said her uncle's words were: "The most important thing you can give children, more important than any material thing you might be concerned about, is a sense of self-confidence." Furthermore, he had told her, if she could give her children confidence in themselves, they would be able to get all the other things they needed for themselves.

As we sat on the beach and thought about Sally's uncle's words of wisdom while our children played together in front of us, I know we wished very much, as probably all other parents do too, to be able to give our children self-confidence.

I have spent much of my effort and thought, as a mother, teacher and counselor, building self-esteem in children because self-esteem seems to be the foundation of self-confidence. Perhaps both words describe the same quality.

Self-esteem doesn't mean overconfidence. When you have healthy self-esteem, you know yourself and accept yourself with your limitations; you are not ashamed of your limitations but simply see them as part of the reality you are, perhaps as a boundary you're challenged to expand.

Building healthy self-esteem is related to loving. Each way of building self-esteem in children presented in this book is also a way of loving. Using these principles, you'll get in touch with a special transforming force within you, a personal loving force that can energize your experience and help you create an atmosphere of love around the children in your life.

A loving atmosphere is necessary for everyone. No one can live healthily for long without loving and being loved. As a primary-grades teacher, I was conscious how a loving environment could be generated when I nurtured self-esteem in children. I also began to be conscious of how a lack of self-esteem and experiences that damaged a child's self-image could interfere with a child's ability to learn and relate. As I continued to observe and reflect upon the children I knew and the children I was coming to know, including my own children, I became more and more aware of the subtle but powerful influences self-esteem, or the lack of it, could have on a child's healthy development. Keeping self-esteem alive is as necessary for each human as water is for plants. Self-esteem is the daily food of emotional health.

Healthy self-esteem is a capacity to see oneself as valuable and competent, loving and lovable, having certain unique talents and a worthwhile personality to share in relationships with others. Far from being conceited or self-centered, it means having a realistic awareness of oneself and of one's rights. It means to honor one's uniqueness and, spiritually, to accept one's life as a gift from God. Because people with healthy self-esteem are usually self-confident, they are able to build healthy relationships, see themselves as successful, and act toward others in nonthreatening ways.

In contrast, people with low self-esteem usually have a negative self-image and a poor self-concept, which hinders their ability to build relationships, to feel unthreatened, to feel successful, to experience kinship with the world, to express their assertiveness, to deal with fear and other strong emotions, and to share their own love with others.

Lack of self-esteem and a negative self-image are reflected in failure-oriented people, those who downgrade themselves. How sad it is to talk to a child who is so afflicted! As a diagnostic tutor, I remembered one such conversation: "What's your favorite sport?" I began with a smile.

"Baseball," he answered unsmilingly. "But I don't play very well."

"What's your next favorite?"

After considerable thought he answered, "Ice skating, but I'm not any good at it." He gave a weary sigh.

"What's your best friend's name?" I asked, hoping to touch a happier interest area.

"Chuck, but he moved away. None of the other guys seem to like me."

Like many people with low self-esteem, this child saw himself as a failure in sports and unsuccessful in friendship. For him, words that described his self-image included inadequate, incompetent, unlovable, unapproachable, and unpopular. He felt demoralized and depressed, and lacked the self-confident courage to try again.

In school a child like this often hides lack of self-confidence behind a mask of bossy and aggressive behavior. In my experience as a counseling tutor, dealing with self-images of children, their parents, teachers, and other people in their environment, such as administrators and family doctors, I became aware of how important self-esteem was to the effective functioning both of children themselves and of those around them.

Not only does the social environment affect such children, but the children affect their environment. An angry and frustrated child touches off anger and frustration in the family and at school. And as people reinforce a child's negative image, for example, saying he is a "difficult child," the child's self-esteem drops lower and lower, while their frustration grows. At the same time, the self-esteem of people around a "difficult child" diminishes as their frustration grows; they feel increasingly inadequate in dealing with the needs of such a child and his or her environment. Situations like this often start a destructive cycle where everyone involved continues to lose self-esteem.

Another important point to remember throughout is that building self-esteem is a process, usually a slow one. Patience and perseverance are important qualities in parents, teachers, therapists, and all other caring adults who want to help build self-esteem in the children under their care. There seems to be a kind of innate drive in children to want to be loved, valued, and esteemed, and to love, value and esteem others in turn. At times I find it difficult to trust that inner drive, but when I watch children in process over a period of time I discover that drive is always at work.

As an adult, I am responsible for being both a teacher and a learner. Children teach me how to teach them, how to help heal them, how to guide and counsel them. They draw creative responses out of me. It's in the interaction with them that my creativity develops and that I learn mothering, teaching and counseling.

All of us, adults and children, are interrelated in a huge network of emotional and spiritual energy. Each one of us is inextricably involved in the stream of life, and the exciting thing is that we can influence its path. Each of us is capable of having positive and negative effects on the emotional and spiritual ecology of the human family. Each of us has the opportunity of sharing love and of helping build that family. To enhance a child's self-esteem is to be a positive force in loving relationship and thereby make a worthwhile contribution to the world.

Building Self-Esteem in Children

I

Building Relationships

One of the first steps in encouraging healthy self-esteem in children is to establish good relationships with them.

Persons in relationship are ultimately what the world is all about. Relationships which are mutually loving and caring, honest and supportive create an atmosphere for healthy human growth.

This chapter's eight principles for nurturing self-esteem in children focus on building such relationships. Principles in later chapters also help foster healthy relationships, but these first eight are very basic ones.

1 ★ Be Available to Children

When I agree to be available to a child, I try to remember to present myself in such a way that the child knows I choose to be available specifically to him or her for this period of time.

For me, when one of my daughters comes to be with me, this may mean hanging up the telephone, turning off the television, putting down my pen, or closing the book or newspaper I may be reading.

Or I may want to state a precise time when I will be able to be with her. "I want to finish this page," I might say. "Please give me five minutes and I'll be able to stop and be with you."

My daughters usually find me sitting at my desk. I used to continue writing as I listened to their latest adventures. I don't know how often it was asked in different ways, but finally one day I think it was Miranda I heard saying, "Please stop writing, mom, so I can talk to you."

"It's okay," I replied casually. "I can keep writing while I listen to you."

Obviously, she didn't believe I could keep listening as deeply as she wanted me to. And the truth of the matter was I probably couldn't. What I usually did with my daughters was listen to their first few sentences. From this I could grasp the gist of their message and decide how important it was. I guess I usually decided what they had to say wasn't all that important, since it was probably more of the usual schoolgirl chatter or gripes.

What I discovered that day was maybe the content of the conversation wasn't that important to her either. Primarily, she wanted me just to listen to her.

It's surprising I had forgotten that, for I find it's just as important for me to be listened to by the people I approach.

Children appreciate not only your availability, but also your full attention. I realized once I stop being busy and become totally present to a child, whether it's for five minutes or five hours, I'm giving them prime-quality time. And that helps build self-esteem because my total attention to them clearly affirms their value to me.

Being available to children sometimes also involves going places and sharing things. For example, parents who take the time to attend events where their children perform, like Little League games, are saying something to their children about how important such sharing is.

One day my niece Laura told me she was going to be in the

May Day Celebration at school. She was to be one of the May-pole Dancers.

"I'd love to come and see you," I said.

"Oh, it's not really anything very big and you're probably very busy. Besides, it's a long drive."

"No, I'd like to come," I told her. "I'll make time to come."

Since she wasn't sure how impressive she would be, what I needed to do was reassure her I wanted to see her dance, and it wasn't important how good the performance would be or how big a role she had in it. Rather, I stressed, it would give me an opportunity to come and share something with her. For her to perform and for me to appreciate it would be a very special shared experience. The sharing was more important to me, I assured her, than the quality of her performance.

What's important to children can be important to me just because it's important to them. And I try to make myself available when opportunities for sharing something are present.

Self-Esteem Principle: Children's self-esteem grows when they know you care enough to be with them.

2 ★ Listen without Making Judgments

In relating to children who want to talk about what they're doing and how they're feeling, stay present to them while they sort out what they want to do or say. Stay with them mentally without offering advice. Be simply a good listener while their initial surface feelings and responses finish pouring out. Without judging them, reflect back to them what they say to you. Give back descriptive words to express what they experience. This kind of nonjudgmental listening proves you value them and their feelings.

One day Julie came home from school, violently burst through the front door, threw her coat angrily on the chair, and without a word stomped up the stairs to her room and slammed the door closed behind her. The emotional exhaust she left in her wake indicated she was either outraged or embarrassed or angry. Or all three.

My first impulse was to be irritated at her behavior and to tell her I did not approve of her violent entrance and impoliteness to me, for she had not even said, "Hi, mom."

On second thought, I realized she seemed angry and upset. Furthermore, I realized the stomping and slamming told me she wanted my attention and sympathy, or she probably would not have made her entrance that way.

I went to her room, knocked on the door, and walked in. I did not wait for her to decide whether or not to invite me in. I saved her the necessity of the decision. Knowing her, she probably would have said, "Go away." In fact, when I walked in the room and found her lying on her bed with her head in her arms, I heard a muffled "Go away," but I decided to exercise my parent's prerogative by sitting down on the bed next to her and gently inviting her to let out her feelings.

At times like these, adults may need a series of questions to ask that are gentler and less abstract than, "What's wrong?" I recall asking Julie a number of questions like, "Did something happen at school? Did something hurt your feelings? Did somebody do something that made you angry? Did somebody hurt you?" and maybe ending up with, "Can you tell me about it?"

"I don't want to talk about it," was her reply.

"I'm sorry something has made you unhappy," I said. I remained seated, patiently and quietly. I hoped she felt my message, that I was content just to offer her my presence as a gesture of comforting. I wanted her to know I wasn't abandoning her and I wasn't uncomfortable with her feelings.

In a little while she began to talk a bit about what had happened. I didn't push for more, I just listened quietly and attentively. It was important for me to let her anger pour out in whatever way it came. It was not necessary for me to try to make any sense of it, not important to point out any of her irrationality, not important to offer any advice about what she should have done or could have done. At that moment my way of loving her was just to listen and let all the confusion, anger, and strong feelings come out in her own words, even if the words she used appeared a bit crude, rude, and probably exaggerated. She even used some words on our family taboo list, but I felt this wasn't the time to remind her of that.

At times she seemed to need help with finding more precise words to describe her feelings and the situation, so I offered some suggestions, not as judgments or conclusions, but rather as a way to help her better express her feelings.

When upset children have as much time as they need to pour out their story in their own way and supply all the details in their own style, they usually feel respected and valued. Julie knew I was taking her seriously and would give her all the time she needed. In an unhurried atmosphere, she could begin to bring herself to some realistic conclusions about the situation and own her own part in it.

Later, when she had calmed down some, I encouraged her to come up with alternatives and evaluate what she wanted to do about the situation, using her own rational abilities.

Julie's situation that day was rather complex. It seems she had been passing notes in class with a few other girls. One of her notes was intercepted by the teacher, who decided, without thinking and without checking it, to read it aloud to the class. As I recall, it said something like, "I think this is the dumbest class I've ever been in and the stupidest teacher in the world." Naturally, Julie was very embarrassed to be singled out in front of the class. I think part of her outrage was that the entire class now knew what was in the note. On top of that, the teacher said, "I want to speak to you after class," at which time she scolded Julie at length; for the teacher too had been surprised and embarrassed hearing herself read the contents of the note.

I listened, supported, and comforted her as best I could, and left what she would do about the situation up to her. I think she realized one of her options would be to write the teacher a note of apology.

I never asked her again about the incident. She knew I was concerned and had listened to her story, she also knew I would let her do what *she* chose to do and not cross-examine her about it. I respected her need for dignity. Till this day I don't know what she did.

Self-Esteem Principle: Listening heals broken self-esteem; healthy relationships develop between children and adults who listen.

3 ★ Remember Names

For teachers, therapists, and concerned friends, it builds self-esteem in children when you show you care enough to remember not only *their* names, but the names of their pets, family members, places they told you about, and other significant details about them. Familiarity with concrete names shows you were really listening and you really understood.

For parents, it's important to remember names of your children's playmates and special classmates, including important details about them, such as the kinds of pets they have and their pets' names. It was important to my children that I got the names of their friends straight, which wasn't necessarily easy at the beginning since some names sounded a lot alike, such as Marcy, Mandy, and Maggie; or Elise, Risa, and Lisa. I remember addressing one of my daughter Julie's friends by the wrong name, and she told me it upset her. (Probably more than it upset her friend.)

As a diagnostic tutor and later as a therapist, I found it made an impact on children when I remembered not only names of their brothers and sisters, but also which was older and which was younger. Remembering such details indicated to these children that their lives were real for me and that I found details about them important. They could tell I had a grasp of the family territory that formed their living space and affirmed it as real and important to me.

I remembered Tommy, a child I worked with in therapy, who told me he took his dog Pepper and his little brother Timmy to play in Glover Park. Weeks later, during a therapy session, I reminded him of these details and said I had thought of him and even looked for him when I had walked my dog in Glover Park the past weekend. It made Tommy feel very special.

My words had affirmed that he kept living in my thoughts even when we weren't in session, that he didn't cease to exist for me when he stepped outside my office door, that he had a place in my life. It made him feel valuable to realize I knew a bit more of who he was in the larger setting of his family and friends.

When I work with children, I like to remember stories they tell me, including some of the details; and I like to mention these stories to them at a later date when some statement comes up that triggers my memory. For example, I might remind a child, "Isn't that the little town where you told me you saw a play you really liked when you were at camp last summer?"

When a child has told me about a dream, and months later I say, "That reminds me of the dream you told me about where you were being chased by a shark," it obviously has a special effect on the child because my remembering reminds them the details of their life they share with me are important to me.

When I not only recall dreams a child tells me but also make connections among those dreams—"I remember another dream you told me about being chased, except then it was a bear chasing you"—it seems to be especially powerful. I am remembering things important to them, and by doing so I validate them in a larger context.

Self-Esteem Principle: Children are enhanced by the network of people, things, and events that make up their lives. When you accept children *in their network,* you most fully accept *them.*

4 ★ Keep the Sharing Mutual

If as parent or teacher you are always the listener, children don't get a chance to show acceptance of you. One-sided sharing fosters inequality in relationships. Both sides in a relationship need to be listeners *and* listened-to.

For example, my daughters come home from school and tell me all their gripes. It might be that sometimes children feel all they do is complain. I find it helpful to let my children know I complain, too, both as a teacher and a parent. I feel comfortable allowing my children to know some of my own gripes, especially those which give them a sense I understand their feelings.

Perhaps more important is to keep sharing mutual when a child is embarrassed about something he or she has done, like Julie and her intercepted note. It is one thing to be generally accepting and to say, "I know how you feel." It is another important step to reveal a similar experience you had. With Julie I was able to say, "I remember once in school walking down the hall, loudly mimicking and complaining about a teacher to a friend, only to discover when I turned around that the teacher was walking right behind me."

Julie immediately wanted to know the details of this embarrassing encounter: "What did you say? What did your friend do? What did the teacher do?" After I supplied these details, she added, "Gee, that must have been awful."

A child needs to be able to recognize you, too, have embarrassing moments in your life and you are willing to talk about them. It steadies a child's tottering self-esteem to know adults share some of their same fears and embarrassments.

In counseling students I've often found myself telling stories about some similar happening in my own student experience that enables the young person to sympathize with me. Perhaps what I am aiming for in this is precisely to allow the child to comfort me. Giving comfort builds the child's sense of competence as a caring, relating person.

I remember coming home one day and telling my daughter Wanda how dumb I had felt having left my car in neutral gear when I hurried into the drugstore. The car had rolled out into the middle of the street, and when I came out of the drugstore, I saw a policeman and another man trying to push it over to the side, out of the way of the traffic that had been held up. I repeated my feelings of stupidity and embarrassment.

"Poor mom," Wanda replied, "that sort of thing can happen to anybody. Don't feel badly."

Wanda's words were very comforting to me, and it made her feel good to have comforted me.

I remember once telling one of the college students my daughter was sick with mono and I was really worried about her. The student had a chance to tell me what she knew about mono, since she once had it and knew other young people who had had it. My sharing gave the student a chance to be informative as well as concerned, comforting and reassuring, as well as be an interested listener. After our discussion, I became a more real person to her and she became more real to me, for I had not experienced the "teaching" qualities of this student before.

In mutual sharing children get an opportunity to feel helpful and valuable to you. In the sharing you become more valuable to them as well, for they know you in a new way. They experience you not only as knower and listener, but also as known and listened-to.

Self-Esteem Principle: Children's self-esteem grows when they know you value them enough to share some part of yourself with them.

5 ★ Emphasize Similarities

As much as possible, especially at the outset of a relationship with a child, find places, ideas, and people you share. Show how you are not separate from each other, but connected.

When dealing with low-self-esteem children, go into their world first to find connections. Find places in their world where you are also at home or with which you are, at least, familiar.

As a tutor trying to build good relationships with children referred to me, I was very conscious to locate similarities at the outset of our time together. The child and I might both have had dogs as pets or had brothers. The television programs these children watched I could say were the same ones I or my daughters watched.

The more significant and personal such similarities are, the more helpful they are in building a trusting relationship. This was especially true when I could talk about things I had done that were similar to things they had done. "When you were little, did you ever fight with your brothers?" or "Did you ever get in trouble?" were typical probes children sometimes made to see just how similar I might be to them.

Both my students and my own children very clearly wanted to know experiences I had had when I was their age. They used to delight in my telling them stories about how I had teased my brothers and fought with them, and about the mischief I had got into. "Tell us about your brothers," they would say. I think their wish was not so much to hear stories for the story's sake, but was to have me share experiences and feelings similar to ones they were having with their siblings. For us, laughing together meant laughing at similar experiences, which, though decades apart, brought about a mutual acceptance and valuing.

When I worked with children in counseling or tutoring situations, I often carried a long list of "favorite" questions: What's your favorite television show? Your favorite dessert? Your favorite ice cream flavor? Your favorite holiday? Your favorite game? Your favorite color? etc., etc. Using these questions, I could begin to uncover similarities between a child and me and help make us feel we had something in common.

Searching for similarities sometimes turns up connections that reach back into our roots. Finding such connections helps build self-esteem in children, for it gives them a sense they are somehow larger than the present moment.

Mrs. Novak was a little old woman who lived down the street from us. In chatting with my children as they walked our dogs, she learned their grandfather lived in Cincinnati. Mrs. Novak had lived in Cincinnati as a child, too. It turned out one of her childhood friends had been a great-aunt to my children; in fact, Mrs. Novak had even known their grandmother when they were both children. This discovery was very special to my children because they had never known their grandmother; she had died when their father was very young. It was special because they got to hear about their grandmother from someone who knew her as a young girl in school—just like them.

After this discovery, my children would visit Mrs. Novak once a week, ostensibly for cookies and milk. Much more important, they were finding similarities between grandmother and themselves. At cookie time conversation inevitably focused on what life was like in Cincinnati when she and grandmother had been little girls.

Every year my children took Mrs. Novak a May Day basket. I don't think my children had ever thought about May baskets before. In fact, they first learned about them from Mrs. Novak. It seems when she was a little girl in Cincinnati, on the first of May children would give little baskets of flowers to people who were special to them. When Mrs. Novak told them about May Day baskets, they told me they wanted to give Mrs. Novak one. And they did. In fact, they continued the custom for three or four years, enough to have shared a special similarity to the grandmother they would never have met, except through the sharing with Mrs. Novak.

While Mrs. Novak had made another dimension of their history real to them and built their self-esteem, they had made her feel important and valuable. The time they spent with her was obviously enjoyed by all. They were always welcome at her house.

Mrs. Novak and my children shared another similarity. They all had dogs. They used to talk about their dogs, especially the problem of keeping their dogs from breaking loose in the neighborhood. Similar problems often give people a sense of relatedness to each other.

Self-Esteem Principle: Children's self-esteem grows when they feel a sense of oneness with other people they like and admire.

6 ★ Care Enough to Prepare

Before a meeting with a child, prepare for it, be ready for it. Bring something to the encounter—an object, a thought, an experience—that shows you were thinking about the child beforehand. This achieves at least three positive self-esteem effects.

First, the something you bring provides an object upon which you both can focus, a meeting place for minds. When I worked with children as a tutor or therapist, I used to look for such a focus of interest. Janie, for example, was interested in the plight of the baby fur seals who are fast becoming an extinct species. I became interested in them from Janie's telling about them. When I'd see an article on Greenpeace or something which referred to the seals' plight, I would bring it to her and say, "I thought you'd be interested in this." Such a focus of interest usually got our sessions off to a good start.

Second, bringing something to the encounter indicates the child is thought of at other times. As a teacher and child therapist, I used to bring things I thought the children might find interesting. They could tell I was thinking of them at other times than our scheduled sessions because the objects I brought were not just things of the moment. Rather they were objects I knew would interest a particular child, motivate him or her and help our work together. These objects and the time I put into finding them indicated clearly the children were on my mind at other times. They and their needs were a reality in my life.

Third, in the very object or item you bring to an encounter as a focus of interest, you recognize a certain uniqueness in a child. This item specifically was selected to be shared. It was something you felt would amuse, interest, or excite them as individuals. As items to be shared I remember bringing a prism, a rock collection, an unusual kaleidoscope that belonged to my children, and a trick box which could make a penny disappear. Kenny in particular was fascinated with magic. I once found a book of simple magic tricks for him, tricks he could actually perform. His interest in magic was something uniquely his. I affirmed him by showing my interest in finding books on magic for him to explore and foster his interest. I also affirmed his valuing of magic, for I told him stories of magic shows I'd seen, and when he told me about magic shows he'd seen, I would listen.

Using this principle with my students provided a complementary self-esteem boost to my own children. In struggling to find an effective way of relating to a very shy, tiny, and withdrawn little girl, I remembered how much my children enjoyed making nests for themselves and friends, using blankets, quilts, and pillows from my bed. One day at the clinic, I found some old blankets, quilts, and pillows and made a nest for the shy little girl in therapy. Because I had known the nest had been interesting (and safe) for my children, I thought it might prove appealing to my tiny patient. And it did.

I made a point of telling her that watching my children build nests made me think she might enjoy it, too. This gave her a variety of affirming messages: that I thought about her outside the therapy room; that I thought about her even when I was with my own children; that I wanted her to have pleasant experiences; that I wanted her to have the same kinds of fun my children had.

The other side of the story, however, happened when I told my children how watching them had inspired me to try some of their creative play with a child patient of mine. When I told them how successful nest building had been, they felt very proud they had been able out of their fun and play to have inspired me and given a healthy experience to one of my patients. As far as I can tell, everybody's self-esteem grew in that exchange.

After that, my children began to feel a part of my tutoring and therapy work. They would suggest games they enjoyed playing that I might want to share with my patients. They also recommended movies and books they liked. In doing this they felt important. Their self-esteem grew as they sensed they had a valuable contribution to make in my work with other children. They also knew they remained present to me while I was at work. Often I told them I remembered something they had said and had used it in a therapy session. From this they knew they were a constant resource for me in my work.

Self-Esteem Principle: Children's self-esteem grows when they know adults share their focus of interest.

Children's self-esteem increases when they know the relationship with you goes beyond the moments of encounter and that you carry their interests and presence with you.

Children's self-esteem grows when their uniqueness is recognized and valued.

7 ★ Take Children to Special Places

Make visiting special places a part of your relationship with children. Take them to a place outside the regular or prescribed structure. Take them to a place you say is special to you so that the memory of it will be of a special place shared.

When I tutored students, I would sometimes take a child to the nearby library, tell them this was the library I used, and explain how I would like to give them an opportunity to come there, too. (I had to get explicit permission to take children, one at a time, from the school grounds, so visiting the library was obviously a special event.) When I said it was my library, it brought about a good sense of connectedness. "Mrs. Berne cared enough about me to take me by myself to her library."

When we were at the library, I'd say, "If you find a book you're really interested in, we can take it out on my library card." This showed not only that I valued them enough to take them to my library, but that they were so special I would let them use my card. It was such a little thing for me to do and such a special thing for them.

By the way, I never cross-examined them about books they took out. I never asked if they had read them. Checking up on their performance was not on my agenda. My purpose in taking them to the library was to help build a relationship of closeness and trust between us. I tried never to set them up in a situation where they could feel there were unclear expectations and that they had somehow failed me. Dealing with expectations will be treated more fully in chapter 3 on nurturing success, but I feel it's important at least to mention it here. With library books I did have one expectation I made very clear: that we return the books to the library, which we did cooperatively by my asking them for the books in plenty of time.

In trying to build self-esteem in children using this principle, it produces powerful effects if you can focus on one child at a time. In tutoring and in therapy work, this is usually possible. With teachers and mothers it is often difficult, but it can be arranged. For example, mothers can prescribe certain times to be alone with each child so that opportunities for one-to-one closeness are encouraged. When I taught in a classroom, I discovered there are ways to work one-to-one with children who need special help. Such ways can be as simple as asking a child to help you carry something to the storeroom or to the office; sitting down next to a child for a few minutes to discuss his or her artwork or a story; falling into step with a child and clearly choosing to walk with him or her to some destination; sharing your lunch with a particular child. When a child accepts a sharing experience with you, the child almost has to accept himself or herself as having special and unique value, at least during the time of the shared experience.

My daughter Wanda and I went together to visit an old inn in Oxford, Maryland. I had heard about the place and had gone there by myself some months before. In telling Wanda about it, she became interested and wanted to go there, too. It had been a special place for me and I was delighted to share it with her. It was important that I made reservations long in advance so we could have the room we wanted. I found that if you're going to take the time to share something special, also take the time to make as sure as possible things will be the way you would like them to be. When Wanda and I went to Oxford together, it proved to be a very intimate, growing-together time for us.

This self-esteem practice of taking children to special places is one that children pick up on and use themselves. I remember taking my daughters to a place on Cape Cod that we came to call the Hidden Garden. This was an old-fashioned garden surrounded by a white picket fence behind an antique shop. I had enjoyed sharing this secret garden with them. What I discovered later was it became the special place to which they took their friends. They had learned sharing a special place, like sharing a special gift, builds self-esteem.

Another thing which sharing a special place brings is esteem for the *relationship*. Each time you do something that builds self-esteem in a child, you are also building esteem for the relationship between you. In other words, the relationship develops a clearer self-image and its value becomes enhanced.

I find very precious those shared experiences my children plan to pass on to their children. My children often remind me of the times I used to take them outside on warm summer nights to look at the stars. We lived in the country then. We'd sit wrapped in blankets against the coolness of the night air. We could hear frogs croaking in the pond. Whenever we saw shooting stars we would make wishes.

My children vividly remember those nights as very special shared occasions, and they talk about wanting to share night stars with their children (when they have them). They talk about it as a kind of gift-experience they hope to pass on through generations. I had learned it in my own childhood. I remembered how watching stars generated a very magical kind of feeling, and I wanted my children to be aware such wonderful things were here in the world waiting to be experienced and shared. If you have places and experiences that are special to you, please share them with your children. Whether it's nature, music, dancing, drama, art, or science, please pass on your gift-experiences to the next generation.

When you share your special places and experiences with children, you invite them into your world in a unique way. Sharing says to them, "I think you're not only unique and valuable to me, but you are also someone like me who would enjoy this experience. I care about you in a way that makes me want to delight you." In response to this, the child's self-esteem grows and the child says, in effect, "Your wanting to delight me must mean I'm worthwhile to you."

Self-Esteem Principle: For children to accept a unique experience with an important person is to accept themselves as important and valuable.

8 ★ Be Real and Don't Pretend

When relating to children, be open and be unapologetically yourself as much as possible. This does not mean you must violate your right to privacy and reveal *everything* you feel and do. No. Being real with children means there is no need to wear a mask. Any pretense or lack of honesty with them is usually quickly perceived. Once dishonesty is discovered or uncovered, all else in a relationship is held suspect.

First of all, being real means you don't have to pretend you know more than you do. You are not obliged to have answers to all the questions children ask. Believing you always have to have an answer to a child's questions puts a heavy burden on you. It also gives the child an unrealistic idea of what it means to be an adult. A child might reason like this: "If adults seem to have all the answers, and that's what it means to be an adult, how am I ever going to become an adult? There are a lot of things I don't know and a lot more things I don't seem to be able to be interested in knowing."

Another benefit in being able to tell a child you honestly don't know something is the mutual trust implied: "I can tell you I don't know something, and you'll still respect me."

Still another benefit in being real is the opportunity it often offers you in guiding the child to a resource where the answer can be found, or in doing the research together. A child in my class once asked me where Springfield was, saying he had met someone from there. "Is it far away?" he asked.

"I don't know," I answered. "Would you like to get out a map? Then let's see if we can find Springfield."

Sometimes it's difficult to give honest responses to low-self-esteem children, especially when, for example, they bring cookies they made or a picture they drew and say, "You won't like the cookies" or "I'll bet you think it's a messy picture." Instead of getting hooked into delivering a critical evaluation of cookies, drawings, or other creations, you can respond to their warm intent, their thoughtfulness, the effort they put into the work. You might try saying something like, "That's very thoughtful of you, and I really appreciate it. You probably took a lot of time to do it. That you thought of sharing it with me makes me very happy."

I found I could honestly share my sad feelings with some children I tutored. One day as I came into the room and sat down with Tommy, aged ten, I said, "hello," but the usual enthusiasm in my voice was missing; so was my usual smile. I found it difficult to stay attentive to Tommy's lesson. I was distracted and quiet, not making my usual encouraging comments, giving flow to the session and positive feedback to Tommy, which was part of my normal style. Soon I began to sense a distractedness in Tommy, too, and a concern he had about his performance. I realized Tommy was reacting to my mood. The problem was a lack of clarity in understanding our relationship that day.

What had happened at my home that morning was that our fourteen-year-old dog Willie had died, and I was really upset. When I came into the tutoring room, I was aware I was still quite sad inside. Tommy picked up on my unusual quietness and lack of enthusiasm. Like many low self-esteemers, he probably thought he was the cause of my bad mood. Instead of continuing the tutoring, pretending nothing was wrong, and struggling alone with my sad feelings, I decided to tell Tommy what was going on inside me.

I told him about how we'd had this old cairn terrier named Willie for fourteen years and how I'd found him dead on the kitchen floor this morning, having died in his sleep. Tommy, of course, remembered seeing Willie, because several times I had brought the dog with me to school. I explained to Tommy I was distracted today because I felt very sad. "It's hard for me to keep my mind on the work you and I are doing because my mind keeps going back to Willie."

Tommy was very helpful to me in asking about my feelings, so I could let them out. He wanted to know if I had cried and if my children had cried. In response to his questions, I was able to talk about my sense of loss. When he wanted to know if we would get another dog, I got in touch with my unwillingness even to think about trying to replace old Willie.

Tommy, in turn, had an opportunity to talk about his fear of loss, for he had a dog. He also revealed his curisoity about death. The session became a time for Tommy and me to become very real people to each other.

Self-Esteem Principle: If children feel *you* are real, then perhaps they can let some of the *real them* show.

II

Being Nonthreatening

Emotionally, children are easily threatened by anyone bigger, older, or more confident than they are. Not yet possessing the well-developed defenses adults usually have, children's sense of self is still fragile, vulnerable, and easily knocked down. For example, children often don't understand the significant difference chronological age can make in their performance. Younger children may feel stupid because their older siblings appear smarter. They do not realize older children have had more time than they for learning skills, physical growth, greater muscle control, more practice, and more experience in sports, school, the arts, and so on. Younger children need to understand they may be years behind in experience but not necessarily in intelligence.

Even without threats from others, low self-esteem children tend to think of themselves as unlovable, incompetent, unimportant, and in the way. Feelings of insecurity, embarrassment, failure, and fear abound inside them.

The nine principles in this chapter point out likely areas where children feel their self-esteem particularly threatened and suggest ways to relate to a child that minimize such threats.

9 ★ Be Careful about Challenging Fantasies

Let children do their own weaning from fantasy. When reality asserts itself, as it will in its own healing time, they will respond to it. Here I'm thinking of the kind of fantasy, for example, where a child talks about fears over a performance. How many times I remember my children coming to me full of apprehension. "I'm going to be in a play, mom, and I know I'll really make a mess of it. Everybody else will be good and I'll be awful. I'll never learn my lines."

Instead of contradicting the fantasy and arguing the child will do fine, which only heightens the child's feelings that you don't understand the magnitude of the problem, you might instead, after reassuring the child you have faith in them, *offer some concrete support,* perhaps volunteering to help the child learn script lines and going to the performance.

Fantasies like these reflect primarily the question of self-esteem. Children are calling for you to recognize how important the task (play, exam, etc.) is to them and how great the fear of failure looms. The caring adult can, first, value those feelings and then show a willingness to help the children deal with the demands of the task. When the children's task is over, together you can deal with the reality. If they succeeded, you can rejoice with them. If they barely survived, you can assure them they hadn't done as badly as they thought. If they failed, thereby fulfilling their fear, you can remind them they did survive and are still living and breathing. When reality asserts itself, respond to it.

A second nonthreatening response to a child's fantasy involves *restating their fantasy in terms of reality.* Point to the reality the fantasy portrays and let children assimilate as much reality as they can. There's no need to make them swallow it.

For example, sometimes a child will tell a story that seems like a lie or a distortion. Instead of challenging the truth of the story, it can be helpful to look at the story as a parallel or metaphor of some real concern in the child's current life. For example, Albert once told me his father was going to take him to Disneyland over Christmas vacation. "We're going to stay in the hotel there," he added. "We'll spend a whole week there going on rides and seeing the shows."

The facts were Albert was a poor and physically handicapped seven-year-old and his father, who didn't live with him and seldom came to visit him, was also very poor. Albert had probably heard about Disneyland from some other child at school.

I looked at Albert's fantasy not as a lie but *as a wish,* so I talked with him about how nice it would be to go to Disneyland and to spend all that time with his father. We never talked about the fact that the trip would not happen, but only about how nice it would be. Albert was taking the opportunity to use his creative imagination to its fullest and to enjoy in fantasy what wouldn't happen in the physical world.

His fantasy told me, indirectly but clearly, how much he wished his father would spend more time with him and do special things with him. The father relationship was an important part of Albert's lack of self-esteem and is something I needed to know about and to work on in therapy with him, not by confronting his fantasy, but by recognizing what he missed and wished for in order to build his self-esteem.

A third nonthreatening way of dealing with a child's fantasy is to respond to the *reality of the feeling behind the fantasy,* whether it be fear, joy, confidence, enthusiasm, or something else. Understand the fantasy as a child's way of setting the scene to display an important feeling, or as a way of allowing themselves to express this feeling.

For example, one evening when Wanda was a little child and her father and I had gone out for the evening, she told me the next morning she had been scared by a nightmare and ran to my bedroom, only to find I wasn't there, and how terrifying that was to her. What she didn't tell was that the babysitter was present in the house at the time in another room.

Part of what Wanda described was a child's terror of going

through empty rooms (we lived in a big house) to get to where mother and father are, only to find they aren't there. According to Wanda's version, she walked back through all the dark empty rooms to her room, crawled back into bed, and experienced very frightened, abandoned feelings.

The fact there was a babysitter around was part of the reality, but it was not important for Wanda. What was important in the fantasy was Wanda's childhood fear of facing frightening things like nightmares without the protection of parents, in short, the fear of being abandoned in a frightening situation.

When Wanda told me this story, I didn't face her with the reality that there was a babysitter in the house. It's easy for parents and teachers to challenge a child's fantasies by saying, "But that isn't true" or "That's just not so" or some version of "You are lying." Rather, I tried to step into her world by agreeing, "It must have been very scary to be such a little girl in such a big house and to find your father and I weren't there to comfort you when you were scared."

As a parent, I often find myself in touch with the wish, impossible as it may be, always to be able to protect my children from scary things. And I sometimes share that parental desire with them, saying, "I wish I could be here for you always, but I can't." This is an important reality for grownups as well as children to learn: That as a parent, I wish I could always be there when I'm needed, but I can't always. I tell this to my daughters, for they'll need to remember it, too, when they have children: You can't protect your children from everything scary, and you can't always be there when you're needed, but you do want to be and you do try to be as best you can.

Self-esteem seems to have to do with being valued for your feelings and fears. It grows when children know their fears are accepted as part of who they are. It's as if I had said to Wanda, "I love all of you, including your feelings and fears."

Accepting Wanda's fears and wishing to have been able to comfort her in them, I could esteem myself as a caring, protective parent. I could feel Wanda's esteem of me as well as her esteem of herself.

I sometimes forget to apply my own principles. A few years ago, my daughter Miranda in her adolescent anger told me I was never there when she needed me "all that year when you were so busy studying and being wrapped up in your own interests."

Instead of hearing Miranda's anger and frustration at not feeling valued and how her needs had gone unnoticed, I defended myself. I enumerated the facts. I pointed out all the times I had driven her to music lessons, play practice, and friends' houses. I reminded her of all the nights I had slept at the foot of her bed during the winter when she had been ill. I told her I was frustrated at her poor memory and lack of appreciation. I was so caught up in asserting "reality" that I couldn't hear in her fantasy her request for more attention and her feelings of being neglected. So we ended up angrily shouting at rather than understanding each other.

Self-Esteem Principle: A budding healthy self-esteem doesn't need to be challenged. Don't weed a garden until the plants are strong enough to stay rooted when you pull the weeds.

10 ★ Be Careful with Your Negative Feelings

The main point to remember here is that children in general, low self-esteemers in particular, tend to think they are the cause of their parents' or teachers' negative feelings. So, if you are angry or fearful because of something that happened outside the relationship with this child, keep those feelings out of this relationship. If your negative feelings are very strong and recent, children may be able to sense them, in which case it may be necessary to share enough of the situation with them so they do not feel responsible for your negative feelings.

Young people usually need to be told clearly that they are not the source of your problems.

During the year I did counseling at a women's college, shortly after the move into my new home, I was frequently angry and frustrated by the messes and delays involved in getting my home in shape. I once cleared an entire morning, changing appointments and schedules, so I could stay at home for a plumber who had promised to come. But he never appeared. I waited at home till long after the last minute and was consequently late at the college for the client who had been waiting for me. I was embarrassed about being late. I wanted to take the time to phone the plumbing company to tell them how angry I was, yet I didn't want to delay her. When we sat down to begin the session, my mind was still focused on what I wanted to tell the plumbing company. I was mentally rehearsing the order in which I would list my complaints. I was not functioning very well as a counselor. My responses, when I made any, were perfunctory and not very helpful, so the student seemed confused about how to talk any further about the issues concerning her.

I wisely stopped and said, "Nancy, please forgive me if I seem distracted. The truth of the matter is I *am* very distracted."

She immediately became concerned. "Is there anything I can do?" she asked.

I realized she felt somehow it might be her responsibility to help me. This broke my tension. I found myself laughing as I said, "You could if you were a plumber." Then I briefly explained I had the usual problem over a plumber who didn't show up. It was nothing for anyone to become overconcerned about, but I had let it get to me. When I recognized the truth of that last statement, I was able to focus on Nancy and her needs.

This was a case where an outside source of negative feelings simply needed to be talked about openly in order to keep the relationship with Nancy moving forward without threat. There have been other times when I chose not to describe what was bothering me but would simply say, for example, "Some things have happened today that made me angry. Please know my anger has nothing to do with you."

Some examples of feelings I usually chose not to share with young clients were those sparked by conflicts among the staff or administration of the places where I worked, those that related to my own family, and concerns about my own physical health.

Last spring I felt sure I was developing an ulcer. I didn't share this fear with any of my clients because it is likely a client might feel she or he simply added to my ulcer—"I'm causing Mrs. Berne's ulcer"—and I didn't want that to get in the way of the work I did with my clients.

I did share my ulcer fears with my secretary. It turned out she had similar fears and symptoms. We became a kind of mutual support for one another, comparing symptoms and encouraging each other to see a doctor and have the necessary diagnostic tests done. Being able to share my fear with her allowed me to keep this fear outside of my counseling relationships. (As it turned out, neither of us had an ulcer.)

Related to this concept is a big question parents have about their deepest worries and concerns. Generally stated, it asks: "What should I share or not share with my children? When is sharing appropriate, and when is it really dumping my worries on a child who can't do anything about them?" More particularly, such concerns might be expressed in the following way: "I don't want the children to know their father has an alcohol problem"; or "I'm having a biopsy to see if I have cancer, and I don't want my children to know it"; or "Our marriage is having serious problems, and I don't know what to tell the children"; or "I don't want my children to know I'm seeing a therapist."

There are no hard and fast rules on what's appropriate to

share with children and when to share it. It depends on the child, the child's age, the kind of relationship you have with the child, how your concern might be presented. Each situation needs to be evaluated uniquely.

One question I usually ask such parents is: "Why do you want to share this information and these feelings with your child at this particular time?"

I would like to point out a distinction between *not sharing* certain information (I chose not to tell my young clients about my ulcer fears) and *hiding it* or *pretending it's not true or real*, for example, in a family where one parent is alcoholic and everyone pretends not to know it. This is called a "family secret." At times children are forced into such pretending. When a family secret builds a sense of hypocrisy or deceit among family members—when, for example, family members deny the alcoholism or lie about how it affects them, *even to each other*—there is a denial of reality, which is ultimately harmful to everyone's self-esteem.

Self-Esteem Principle: If low self-esteem children see you in a negative state, they will naturally think you are angry, frightened, etc. because of them.

Low self-esteem children have enough difficulty dealing with their own negative feelings. There is no need to burden them with your negative feelings from other sources.

Share your negative feelings with children only when the sharing, carried out in a spirit of growth, honesty, and authenticity, fosters positive self-esteem and development of the whole child.

11 ★ Be Willing to Reach Out Physically

Whenever children feel threatened, instead of making them come to you, meet them at *their safe place*, and together from there move to new places. Remember, a path is usually neutral territory. Walking to a new place together provides a gentle way of being together, allowing you to grow accustomed to each other.

When I was about to begin tutoring a new child, especially a younger one, I often felt it was important to go to the child's classroom and walk together to the tutoring room, instead of simply having the child come to me. At least for the first couple of sessions, I did this for almost every tutoring client; with very young ones, I did it almost all the time. For the first few sessions, I might even walk them back to their classrooms afterward.

Usually for this walk I would bring some object I thought they might be interested in to help them feel comfortable, especially at the beginning of our relationship.

The first time I went to wait for eight-year-old Sandy, she was so scared her usually pale skin was red with anxiety. As we walked together to the tutoring room, I told her my name and asked her name. Then I asked her where she lived, and she was so anxious she couldn't remember. I quickly went on to another topic so as not to let her stay caught in her embarrassment.

"I have three children," I said. "Do you have any brothers or sisters?"

Haltingly, she said, "Yes." Then I realized the very act of talking was difficult for her in her anxiety about beginning tutoring work.

So I opened my purse and took out a very large prism. I handed it to her, saying it belonged to one of my daughters who was her age. I suggested one of the fun things to do with it (as my children discovered) was to look through it as you walked. So she held the prism in front of her eyes and looked at the changing view as we walked.

She rewarded me with a smiling comment, "That's neat!"

By that time we were at the tutoring room and it was easier

to step into the new place. I suggested she could also look at the window view through the prism. She took time doing that to become comfortable in the room with me. I had a mandate to teach Sandy reading and spelling, but my agenda that day was getting comfortable with each other, not teaching. And in every way I could I reached out and made our time together as nonthreatening as possible.

While her classroom was her safe place, the tutoring room was a new place. The path from the classroom to my room had been neutral territory. I began relationship building in the neutral territory. Not only did I show interest in her, but I wanted to bring physical objects, like the prism, into her life that would interest her. For children, concrete things symbolized my wish to bring new learning experiences into their lives. The prism wasn't just some toy, it symbolized seeing and learning in new ways with different materials. It summarized the kinds of learning that would go on in our sessions.

It's difficult for many adults to remember how threatening almost every new situation is for a child, including going to a new school, a hospital, a doctor's office, a dentist's office, summer camp, etc. Even going to a birthday party at a home the child has never been to before can be anxiety producing.

When, as a parent or teacher, you are taking a child to any new place which might provoke anxiety, instead of rushing the child and hurrying them out the door, make the going as nonthreatening as possible. First of all, give the child time to get ready at his or her own pace. Second, allow time for discussing the experience and describe to the child what the experience will be like in as nonthreatening a way as possible. Third, anticipate some of the questions the child might have but is not brave enough to ask you. You can answer these unasked questions by beginning, "You might be wondering about . . ." Fourth, reassure the child you will physically accompany the child to and from the place.

In all of this let your voice be an instrument of comfort as well as of information. The comforting sound of your voice will have its effect, even if much of your information doesn't make it through the barrier of anxiety.

It is very helpful to allow the child enough time to prepare so as not to feel hurried. The ideal is to have the child feel he or she is being invited to go willingly, that is, supported and encouraged to go, but not forced.

In giving the child enough time, much self-esteem building goes on. The child feels somehow he or she is considered an important enough person to be waited for, that his or her own pace of getting ready is respected. Your wanting the relationship and the situation to be a safe one says the child is valuable to you. Your willingness to be physically present says, "Your security is important to me."

In the process you, the adult, are learning a certain amount of patience and trust in yourself. And the sense of cooperation that's present speaks of a mutual esteem.

Self-Esteem Principle: Self-esteem grows best in children when they have plenty of time in a safe or neutral place to check things out before they finally trust themselves to a new or possibly threatening situation.

12 ★ Hold Encounters in Relaxed Places

Places conducive to relaxation offer better chances for caring relationships to develop, especially if children feel threatened.

When you're about to tell a child something difficult, don't do it in the middle of the playground, the middle of the street, the middle of a classroom, or the middle of a family. If it's something that's personal and perhaps difficult, find a place that feels peaceful and protective, as conducive to an atmosphere of nonthreatening support as possible.

At home, I usually choose the child's room for personal sharing. It's preferable because it's a place that's mostly their turf and feels safe to them.

In school, I take pains to find a quiet place, perhaps the principal's office or the nurse's room (as long as it's unoccupied at the time), so a child can deal with the ensuing fear, hurt, grief, or other feelings without the risk of feeling embarrassed about showing emotions.

For example, I went to the therapeutic nursery to get Hilda, aged four, for her first therapy session. Relatively new in the school, she had been so frightened and withdrawn no one really knew if she could talk, or if she was capable of interacting with children, or with anyone for that matter.

It seemed to me that a trip to my office would be a very long one for Hilda, so instead I chose to use the large playroom directly across the hall from her classroom. I had no idea what I would do with this tiny, frightened girl; when anyone let go of her hand, she wouldn't move, she'd just stand there as if she were frozen. I chose the playroom as the most relaxed and least threatening place I could think of and hoped it offered a good setting for a trusting relationship to develop between us.

Beginnings are often difficult for children. So are endings. Separations and leave-takings are powerfully emotional times.

I discovered Chuck's family was soon to move out of the area, so I wouldn't be able to work with him anymore. I chose to do something special and peaceful for our last session. Ours had been a tutoring-therapy relationship, and Chuck had worked hard at every session. For this final time together, I gathered some colored pens and sketch pads and said, "Let's go across the street to the park. We'll just draw and talk."

We never got around to drawing. We just lay on our backs, looking at cloud formations and talking about the different kinds of leave-taking we had done in our lives and the people we missed. We talked about the fact that we wouldn't see each other anymore. The park and the billowy sky proved to be a gentle, safe, relaxed, nonthreatening place for encountering a difficult experience.

Chuck had had a fear of separations, but his self-esteem grew as he realized he could deal with a separation without having to deny his feelings of sadness and loss. In fact, not only was I willing to listen to his feelings, but I was also willing to share my own, which confirmed that he was valuable to me. Not only would I miss him, I also trusted him enough to tell him about it. He was important enough that I could tell him. His self-esteem as a valuable person was affirmed.

Self-Esteem Principle: At moments when self-esteem seems threatened, children feel more confident when the setting is conducive to feeling cared for and valued.

13 ★ Keep Encounters Predictable

Help children become as familiar as possible with what is likely to happen in an encounter. Predictability reduces fear of the unknown. Knowing what's going to happen allows children to prepare themselves for it, and perhaps to be predisposed to find enjoyment in it. In this way, successful self-fulfilling prophecy is built into the experience.

This principle applies to parents in many ways. For example, let's say parents are having a party and they would like the children to be involved in some way. To keep the encounter predictable, tell the children names of guests who will be present at the party and exactly what you expect the children to do. If you would like them to be around and helpful throughout the party—taking coats, passing hors d'oeuvres, and the like—make sure they know how to do it. Demonstrate, if necessary. If you simply want them to say hello to the guests and then go back to their rooms, tell them so. Also, they appreciate not being surprised by a last-minute change of plans, such as having to dress up in a hurry.

The same kinds of explanations are very helpful to children in building self-esteem and avoiding embarrassment if they know precisely what's expected of them when you take them to weddings, funerals, or any unusual religious or social event.

Even when you're taking a child for a first haircut, describe the procedure and the process to keep any possible surprises to a minimum.

Any medical examination or physical process with which a child is unfamiliar can be thoroughly described and discussed with the child beforehand, for example, menstruation, first gynecological exam, an appendectomy or tonsillectomy, a glucose tolerance test, a blood test, and the like.

Dentists today often tell children, before a dental procedure is begun, what they will do and what the child is expected to do. Then, even if the process gets uncomfortable, it's not as fearful as it could have been had the child not known what to expect.

Teachers often tell students what material an exam is going to cover. It may not be an easy exam, but it's not quite as fearful as it would be if students had no idea what to expect.

Among the children I tutored, academic skills were always a problem and testing was always dreaded. Usually I was only the tutor; somebody else did the testing. But I did whatever I could to keep test surprises to a minimum. I explained who would come and what they looked like, so the personal appearance of the tester would not be a surprise. I described what the test would be like and how long it would take. I might even give them some typical kinds of questions. It also really helped to evoke the child's own questions about the testing process, even if I had to encourage their questions.

And I always assured children I'd talk over the results of the testing at our next meeting (or soon at least) so they were not left wondering and worrying about how well or how poorly they did. Leaving children in doubt about how they did does not help build self-esteem. Low self-esteemers tend to view not knowing in a negative light. For them, no news is bad news. In sharing the results of their testing with them, I esteem their right to know themselves and their performance.

When I am personally going to administer an intelligence test or some other test, especially where the responses are timed, I explain to the children the test is designed for a wide range of children, some of whom are much older than they are: "Some questions may seem very easy, while others seem very hard. Don't be upset if you can't answer all questions; you are not expected to." I usually add, "Nobody can. You'll get some of them, and that's just fine."

Those kinds of comments are one small way of helping preserve a child's self-image. Surprises generate fear, and fear can destroy not only self-esteem, but a child's ability to function well. If children experience themselves as failing—and that's what low self-esteemers tend to do—then any situation offering an opportunity for frequent failure has the potential of demoralizing children and creating a negative self-image rather than a positive one.

When children don't know what's expected of them, they feel awkward, confused, and fearful. For them to feel welcome and accepted and successful in a situation, it helps if they know what to expect.

Self-Esteem Principle: Fear is a great destroyer of self-esteem. Predictability reduces fear.

14 ★ Never Embarrass Children

When relating to children, especially when they feel threatened, let them know they do not have to prove themselves to you. Let them know there are no strings attached to what you do or to what you ask them to do.

I took Tommy, one of my tutoring students, to the library and I let him take out a book, but I never asked him if he had read it. I did not want to put him in the embarrassing position of perhaps having to admit he hadn't read it or didn't like it. Our purpose in going to the library had been to enjoy special time together. I hoped he would find a book he would both enjoy and be motivated to read. I trusted if he'd read the book, he'd spontaneously give me his reactions when he brought the book back, without my having to cross-examine him.

A similar idea applies when you give a child a gift. Wait for their reply before you ask if they like it or are grateful. Basically, asking a child if they like a gift may conceivably put the child in an embarrassing situation, for they may not know how to be honest with you and still give you the polite reply they assume you're asking for. If you need to say something when the child opens the gift, say something affirming like, "I want you to know I love you," or "I was thinking of you," or "It's good to be celebrating today with you."

In itself to be embarrassed is a very uncomfortable experience for any child. To be embarrassed in front of others compounds the feelings. But to be embarrassed in front of one's peers is probably the most uncomfortable.

As a teacher, parent, and therapist, I have always tried to protect children from experiences of embarrassment, even in front of me. Embarrassment is one of the most effective ways to devastate a child's self-image and self-esteem. If a child is a low self-esteemer, embarrassment can completely wipe out their self-esteem, at least for a moment.

At home when one of the children is embarrassed or upset and doesn't want her sisters to see her crying or to know what happened, especially if someone had made her feel stupid or unloved, I feel it is probably wise for me to take time to protect the child's privacy while she deals with her strong feelings. If she wants to tell me about it, I try to make sure we're in a private place where we're not apt to be bothered and others are not likely to see her tears. For this reason, sometimes I've taken an embarrassed daughter into my room and closed the door, and even told her she could stay there as long as she wanted with the door closed so that nobody would bother her. I might even bring her a snack, or do something that might comfort her, like rub her back or brush her hair. In general, my intent would be to help her rebuild the broken pieces of her self-esteem in whatever ways I could.

Self-Esteem Principle: Embarrassment can be very destructive of a child's budding self-esteem.

15 ★ Don't Set Up Tests of Trust

Trusting children seems to be a significant factor in building their self-esteem. Children sense when you're testing them. A test of trust proves there is little or no trust. Rather be confident that mutual trusting, which is an extended process, will grow naturally as your knowledge of each other grows. Trust-growth happens most naturally when you and the child are mutually open, when you don't close yourself off, and when you let your true emotions (especially your positive ones) show.

My daughters, I am told, are rather unique because they usually did their homework without being told. Parents and teachers have asked me how I managed to get my children to do their homework without checking up on them. "How did you motivate them to want to do it and to do it without nagging?" they asked.

I accept no laurels, for the motivating happened quite unconsciously on my part. The fact was I didn't know any better than to trust them to do it. From the beginning, I simply left to them the responsibility for doing their schoolwork. The oldest daughter passed on the awareness to the others, I guess. Since I didn't check up on them, they had to check up on themselves. As it turned out, they were more demanding of themselves than I would have been of them.

While I could argue that the children became responsible themselves for doing homework because in our home academic performance was valued, the dominant cause seemed to be more in terms of my trust: I trusted they knew what they had to do and would do it, that they knew the assignments and when they were due, and would take responsibility for doing them. And they did.

Moreover, each daughter did it in her own style. One's habit was to get assignments done ahead of time, if possible, while another consistently finished at the last exhausting minute, but finish she would.

It's not that my children didn't complain about homework as other children did. I often heard about how difficult and over-whelming their homework felt to them. However, their comments to me seemed more a matter of information than an invitation to get involved, worry about it, or nag them.

I never got to the point, as many mothers have told me about, where I had to bargain and threaten, or where I had to poke my head in the television room half a dozen times each schoolnight to ask, "Have you got your homework done?" Tactics like these tend to put parents and children in an adversary position, and sometimes invite lying in children.

The trust factor looms large during adolescence, when parents hear stories of drugs, alcohol, and sex. I am often wary of parents who confidently talk about being "sure" neither their children nor their friends use drugs or alcohol. What I'm saying is children will be exposed to drugs, alcohol, and sexual opportunities, and since no parents can ever completely protect them from such contact, one of the best things parents can do is convey to their children how much they value them and their health. Tell your children how precious they are to you, tell them you trust them to value themselves and to take care of themselves.

Above all, trust helps keep lines of communication with children open, so they feel free to talk about their questions and concerns. How healthy it is for children and parents to discuss concerns in a nonthreatening, trusting environment, and to laugh together whenever possible.

Self-esteem is nurtured reciprocally by trust. If someone values you, it's important that that person is someone you value. It's helpful when the child values the parent, so that the parent's esteeming of the child nurtures the child's self-esteem.

When an adult cross-examines an adolescent as to "what went on at that party," it's difficult for the child to know if the questioning is happening because the parent values the health and safety of the child, or because the parents are concerned about their own control over the child's life. Such control doesn't mix well with trusting.

However, I think it's very important for parents to recognize the times when valuing and loving a child also call for setting limits and exercising some control. Children can assume responsibility for their own lives only in areas where they are mature enough to do so. Some things involve too much responsibility, and here's where parents need to be sensitive and assertive.

I'm thinking, for example, of the question of setting curfews for young adolescents. Freshmen in high school are often unsure and confused about how to fit in at the new school, how to be popular and accepted by the other students (whose ages span the critical years from early to late adolescence). As a parent, you may feel it's important for the protection of your children to set up guidelines and limits they perhaps would not exercise themselves, for example, getting home before a certain hour from visiting friends or attending sporting and social events.

Even when you discuss things like curfews openly with your children, this does not mean they won't complain about it, even when a final decision is an agreed-upon compromise. Parents need to trust they and the children can healthily survive the times of complaining and limit-testing. Parents may need to remind children caringly that there are very good reasons, having to do with their valuing the children, for the limits and controls that are set. Show children the limit-setting is a clear and well-reasoned decision, not something inconsiderate, or just a display of parental power. I say this because some parents put limits on children without much reflection and without looking at the children's side of the situation. Parents may act somewhat thoughtlessly here because they may be caught up in the familiar sense of needing to protect their children, as if the children were still four or five years younger, or as if one set of rules would appropriately fit all the siblings.

Other parents may set limits for reasons having to do with the parents' own psychological needs, for example, parents who like to be totally in control, or parents who like to regulate their household with a kind of rigorous military discipline and orderliness. Some parents are so fearful of anyone criticizing their children, since it seems at the same time to be a criticism of their "good parenting," that they cannot allow their children much flexibility or normal risk-taking. But even these issues may be talked through and discussed with adolescent children. Admit you're more comfortable when you are in clear control or that you prefer your family to be above reproach, but don't demand that your children live up to *your* preferences.

Showing your feelings and being open with children evokes their trust, and self-esteem grows.

Self-Esteem Principle: In order for threatened children to experience trust, they need to know that showing how one really feels is acceptable.

16 ★ Show Interest in a Nonthreatening Way

Children with low self-esteem are usually eager to relate but fear being able to relate successfully. Since failure is most threatening to them, be positive and success-oriented in your approach.

As I mentioned before, one of my usual approaches in relating to a new child in tutoring or therapy is to have ready a series of nonthreatening questions in neutral areas, for example, favorites or preferences in sports, hobbies, colors, music, holidays, food, etc. Talking about such topics usually fosters relaxed relating.

Direct questions are not always helpful. Often my clients are children who have suffered traumas or serious problems. It requires a delicate balance to show interest in what's bothering a child without sounding as if I were prying or perhaps morbidly curious. Nina, for example, needed to talk to me about her father being killed before her very eyes. For me to have asked direct questions about the killing would have seemed like the nosey neighbors she later told me about who had cross-examined her after her father's death. It took a long time for Nina to trust that I was interested in her and how things were in her life. It took a long time before she realized I was not a threat to her. I had begun relating by focusing on areas like sports and school, which were less threatening. When she was ready, she allowed a deeper relating, where she talked about her family. Only after that did she bring up her father's death.

The principle of showing interest in a nonthreatening way applies also to less extreme examples. For instance, I know some children who are terribly uncomfortable talking about a parent who is ill, especially if the parent is hospitalized. With such children, I find it helpful to show concern in a casual way without making the child feel he or she must go into details, which might make them cry and feel embarrassed, or in any way uncomfortable, for example, "I'm sorry to hear your father's in the hospital. I hope he'll be fine." If a child wants only to reply "Thank you," it's okay for him or her to do so. Or a friendly, neighborly statement like, "I understand your mother is sick. Let me know if there's anything I can do," does not put pressure on the child, yet can be of great help.

Many parents, including myself, are often wondering if their adolescent children need some guidance or help. As parents, it's often difficult to know how to broach subjects like sex, alcohol, or drugs. You want to relate to the children openly and want them to be able to confide in you and to ask *you* questions rather than have their questions or fears go unanswered. I have this wish, too, not only for my own children, but also for the children I tutor and counsel. I've learned to look for the signals they give when they want to talk about something.

At age eleven, Sandy, who wanted to ask questions about her own adolescent development, took to drawing nude women on the chalkboard from time to time during tutoring sessions. I sensed it was a message to me, so I formulated a nonthreatening question. I asked, "Is there something about a woman's body you're specially interested in?"

"No," she said flatly. "I think women's bodies are icky. Icky," she repeated with emphasis.

That was her opening and my cue, so I asked, "Why icky?"

She said, "They get all fat and funny looking." I asked if she meant they developed breasts and sometimes had babies.

"Yes," she replied, "but I'm never going to let *that* happen to me."

"What are you afraid will happen?" I asked.

"I sure don't want *that blood thing* to happen to me," she asserted.

"What do you mean?" I asked. And without waiting, I took a guess, "Do you mean menstruation?"

"Yes," she said. "What if I'm walking down the street with a boy and the blood starts to run down on the ground?"

"Did anybody ever tell you about menstruation?" I asked gently.

"One of my friends did," she replied, "and she said that could happen."

"I don't think it would really happen that way," I assured her. Then I asked her if she would like me to explain how menstruation worked. She said yes, and I did.

After that, she stopped drawing pictures of nude women on the chalkboard.

What was already a trusting relationship between Sandy and me became even more so. During the encounter over menstruation, I kept the situation as nonthreatening as possible. There were only the two of us, we had plenty of time in a private place with no interruptions. I invited her, step by step, into talking about what was troubling her. I respected her privacy and her own way of telling me what she needed. I didn't view drawing pictures of nude women as something to scold her about, but rather I searched for the motivation behind the action. I honored her need to express herself in whatever way her innate creativity would suggest.

It also helps for parents to look for the reasons behind their child's action, as well as at the action itself. When a child is trying to get your attention by behavior, perhaps inappropriate or negative behavior, you can be sure there is usually some reason or issue behind it. A repeated behavior indicates the issue is pushing to be addressed. Maybe part of this self-esteem idea is for you yourself not to be threatened by behavior in your child that appears shocking. Spend your energy caringly probing for the message behind the behavior and its successful outcome.

Self-Esteem Principle: Successful relating with children nourishes self-esteem. And *you* can help provide the conditions for it.

17 ★ Ask Questions That Don't Threaten

Even though asking questions is a very powerful way of building relationship with children, low self-esteem children often feel very threatened by direct questions, especially about their self-image and feelings. When preparing for an encounter with a child, ask yourself: "What will we talk about?" When you select a few topics, formulate some of the questions you might like to ask, then see if they are open-ended. If they are too direct, reformulate your questions in a less threatening way.

For example, in the story of Sandy drawing nude women on the chalkboard, I didn't ask directly "Why did you draw that picture?" or "What's the meaning of this picture?" Even though they were the questions I ultimately wanted answered, in that form they would have immediately put a child on the defensive, especially a low self-esteemer. They would have implied the child had done something hostile or wrong, something which deserved a scolding or rejection, a clear self-esteem deflator.

What I did say merely acknowledged I had observed the obvious: Did she have a special interest in a woman's body? Since she obviously did, it was a nonthreatening question, which led us safely to uncovering things she really wanted and needed to talk about. Each of my questions reflected what she was saying and took us another step in the direction of her concern. My questions and comments were carefully worded so that none of them was accusatory or put her self-esteem at risk. The tone of my voice also conveyed my nonjudgmental interest in her and her feelings, which again protected her self-esteem.

As a parent, if you know you will be encountering your child who, say, has been sent home from school for disciplinary reasons, spend a little time thinking about the questions you plan to ask the child. Out of your caring, decide to find a way to draw out the child's version of the story in a way that won't be accusatory or judgmental. Instead of the usual, "Okay, what did you do?" see if you can ask for the facts in a way that optimally insures the child's sense of security and trust in you. In this atmosphere the child can honestly explain the situation to you without needing to be defensive.

Instead of having the encounter in the front hall, move with the child to a safe place. "Let's go sit in the study (a comfortable and cozy room in our house) and talk about what happened." Your caring tone of voice is very important here.

Once you get settled in the safe place, let the child know what you know about the situation. That usually clarifies the starting point for the child. You might do this by saying, "I had a phone call from the school today. They said they were sending you home because of your behavior. I'd like you to tell me in your own words what was happening. You are very important to me and I would like to hear your side of things. Could you fill me in?"

These first moments are very critical and usually set the tone for the entire encounter, so use phrases—there are usually certain comforting phrases peculiar to each family—that make the child feel comfortable. Ask your questions in a way that does not feel stilted, distant, or awkward. Above all, try not to get hooked into a psychological game called "outraged parent vs. problem child." Consider your various questions beforehand, if possible. You may even try mentally rehearsing them in order to find ways of asking them that are most apt to bring sharing and caring to the relationship.

Self-Esteem Principle: A moment's reflection about the wording of a question may make a significant difference in a child's self-esteem growth.

III

Nurturing Success

Nothing is as effective in building children's self-esteem as success. It even has the power to begin reversing a child's negative self-image. Self-esteem cannot grow healthily without some success to nourish it.

This chapter deals with two basic areas where success is essential to children: success in relating (for example, being loving and lovable, giving and receiving affection, building friendships and social networks), and success in work (for example, being competent, effective, proficient, skillful, and getting things done, especially in school).

The next eleven suggestions offer ways for you to build success into children's lives by finding their existing interests and also capitalizing on previous successes.

18 ★ Build Success into the Relationship

A sense of success grows slowly in children, since they are prone to feeling inadequate around adults. To help children succeed, create situations where failure is least likely. It also helps if you can be alert to their fear, embarrassment, and likely areas of failure. You will learn to notice their hesitancy in such areas. Rather than pushing or forcing them, follow their lead, support and encourage what they want to do, use whatever motivation is present. Instead of trying to change their focus of interest, you might look for ways to support that interest. Often that very interest will supply a way to the desired successful learning and growth.

When I started tutoring Tommy, a nonreader at age nine, his teacher said he was a daydreamer and didn't seem interested in doing anything but drawing pictures. At our first session, I asked Tommy what he liked to do. He said he liked to draw pictures of creatures he dreamed up. I was fascinated, said so, and asked if he would do a drawing for me right then. Sometimes it could take hours and hours to do a single drawing, he explained, as new details continued to emerge in his imagination. I told him we didn't have hours, but we would take half an hour now for a picture.

As Tommy began to draw, I asked him to describe to me what he was drawing and why. A story emerged. A squirrel-like creature decked in Levi's, cowboy hat, and guns was coming through the swinging doors of an old-fashioned western saloon. As he penciled in more details, he elaborated the adventure more and more.

As Tommy drew and talked, I began writing in a notebook the words of his story exactly as he spoke them. When the half hour was over, he had produced a very interesting drawing and a very interesting story; and I told him so. I said I would type out his story and bring it to our next session. We talked about how at our tutoring sessions he could draw a picture and tell a story, and that would be part of our work together. I have a notion it didn't sound like work as far as he was concerned, for he was delighted at the suggestion.

The stories that emerged from the drawings became our first reading materials. (By the way, this was not a new idea. Sheila Ashton Warner in a book called *Teacher* wrote about children creating their own stories to read.) Since the child recognizes his own words, it's easier to learn to read them. And since he's produced the story, the potential for reading successfully is built in. I had taken Tommy's interest, followed it, supported it and, with him, found a way for it to be a basis of our tutoring mandate: for Tommy to learn to read.

From pictures and stories we graduated to the Sears catalogue, which he liked because of the large section devoted to toys. Selecting toys he wanted for Christmas became a tool for learning handwriting and organization skills as he copied information and made out order blanks for the items he liked.

Tommy's story is a success story. In only four months he had gone from being a nonreader to a third-grade reader; he was right up there with his class soon after Christmas. I didn't have a magic wand, but I had acknowledged his wellspring of interest, which seemed to work its own magic for him, enabling his intellectual growth to happen without stopping his creativity.

I had learned from Mrs. Chilton, my first mentor, to recognize realistically what a child can or cannot do. "Be sure you don't ask them to do something beyond their limits in the beginning," she used to say, "because their inevitable sense of failure will make them not want to try a second time."

Mrs. Chilton had taught primary school for more than forty years and claimed she never had a child she couldn't teach to read. (It is only fair to add that she always worked in private schools, where she did not have to deal with highly disturbed or retarded children.) She believed every child could learn to read; it was up to the teacher to find the way in which each particular child could learn. She went on to explain how success breeds success. She stressed how teachers needed to build a sense of success in a series of very easy steps so that a child's self-esteem and self-confidence were functioning optimally on their behalf when presented with each task in the series.

For example, when working with her class on a new story from the reader, she would introduce all the words of the story before the children were presented with the story itself. A little red paperback—called *Fox and Hen,* I think—was the very first reading book she gave her class. It didn't have very many words. Yet before she handed out the books to read, she presented the class with every word—on the chalkboard, on picture cards, on posters—till she was reasonably sure the children were familiar with every word in the book. Lots of little successes were building up among the children. Next, she took one of the books for herself and read the story aloud to the children. Third, she gave each child a book, and as they opened it to the first page, she began to read it again, and the whole class read it with her. Each child felt a sense of success, because the experience of being able to read was present to each one on some level. As I watched, I could see the surprise and delight in the children at being able to read the first book given to them in school! Step by successful step, Mrs. Chilton had led them to and through the task, and certainly their self-esteem was enhanced.

For Mrs. Chilton, to learn was to succeed. She believed in using every opportunity as a positive learning experience. It couldn't have been more than the first or second day of class I worked with her, when a little girl spilled her carton of milk. As soon as the child began to whimper, Mrs. Chilton noticed the child's problem. She calmly but quickly took some paper towels, walked over to the puddle of milk, and addressed the class: "Let me show you how these paper towels can absorb." She then proceeded to give the children a lesson in the process of absorption. The child who spilled the milk, instead of merely being embarrassed at her spilling, could be relieved to know she had provided a special learning for the class. If Mrs. Chilton's quick response didn't enhance the child's self-esteem, it certainly didn't damage it as would have been the case had the child been scolded for the accident and left to the teasing of her peers.

The same success principle applies at home. When you ask

a child to do things, choose tasks *that* child can do successfully, so he or she can enjoy the approval and self-esteem that comes from doing a task successfully. Don't ask young children to set the dinner table without first showing them how. Better, begin one step at a time. Today, ask them only to put out the napkins; show them how to do it for one plate and see that they succeed in doing the rest. Building on success with napkins, you can then invite them to carry out the more complicated arrangements step by simple step.

It's more important that you show children new to a task how you want it done. Then later you won't be forced to say, "That's wrong," or "That's not the way I wanted it done." Showing the way fosters success. If it is not done the way you wanted, you can then gently ask, "Do you want me to show you again?" which is an invitation to cooperation rather than a rejection of their effort.

By the way, you can always thank a child for trying even when the child doesn't fully succeed. Valuing children's efforts also enhances their self-esteem.

Self-Esteem Principle: Success builds self-esteem. It works well every time, and best when the line of successes remains continuous and unbroken.

19 ★ State the Positive Without Evaluating

Recognize what is positive and successful in a child's work or behavior, then acknowledge it by describing what you see and how you feel. Whenever possible, avoid evaluating children, their behavior, or what they do, even if your evaluation is favorable. Typical evaluations include "right," "wrong," "good," "bad," "better," and "worse." Evaluating means judging, and a judge by definition is *above* the relationship, not an equal working side by side. Describing and affirming offers information nonjudgmentally from a positive perspective.

I remember Sandy telling me when I was tutoring her she wished I didn't say "good" everytime she did something correctly because it made her very self-conscious and anxious about the times she wouldn't hear me say "good," which would mean she was doing things wrong. Afraid of what might sound like criticism from me, she preferred I withheld saying "good." So I did. Instead of my comment giving her positive reinforcement as I thought I was doing, in Sandy's case I was actually making her nervous about her performance. What I also found out was Sandy herself knew when she was reading correctly. She didn't need my "evaluation."

I have discovered that some children, and even some adults, are so performance-conscious they can't tolerate even positive feedback without becoming anxious. Usually the anxiety of such children seems to revolve around *pleasing* people, and while their self-esteem is closely tied up with pleasing, so is their anxiety. Consequently, they are apt to get tense and make the very mistakes they fear when the person they want to please continually evaluates their performance, even positively.

Instead of evaluating children or their work, I have found it more successful in building their self-esteem *to describe*. I tell them what I see and how it makes me feel, thus giving them a chance to tell me what they see and how they feel. A sense of equality emerges.

When children draw pictures and show them to me, instead of saying "It's a good picture," I talk about the details of the picture. In this way the child knows I am looking at the picture in depth; talking about it and asking about it is a clearer valuing of the child and the picture than if I just said, "Good," or "That's a nice picture." Sharing reactions to the picture evokes an interaction in the relationship, which enhances self-esteem.

The same principle applies when children show me something they've accomplished, such as wrapping a gift, decorating a cake, or molding something out of clay. I can talk with them about the effort they put into the work, the choice of materials, the choice of subject matter, the choice of colors or shapes or lines, and the details in the work that specially reflects them and their creativity. All of this is a validation and affirmation of them, and not merely an evaluation of their product. Validation provides a more direct nourishing of self-esteem.

Here we're talking about taking the time to be with the child, not just dismissing the child and the product with a glance and a perfunctory comment.

Many times my own children as well as students have come to me saying something like, "I want to show you something I made, but I'll bet you won't like it and you'll probably think it's dumb." When I simply say, "No, I like it," I often hear back, "Are you sure?" or "You're not just saying that?" I find it important for me to take the time to say not only what I think but also why. I find this especially important regarding my children's appearance, such as what they choose to wear and how they choose to do their hair.

"How do you like my hair this way, mom?" Miranda asked one day. I noticed she had moved the part in her hair an inch to the right.

"I think it looks very nice," I replied. Becoming more specific and explanatory, I added, "It doesn't look too different from when you parted it in the middle, though it does change the shape of your face a little now that I look at it longer."

"Makes my face look too fat, doesn't it?" she suggested disappointedly.

Again, instead of simply saying yes or no or evaluating her appearance, I dealt with her question honestly. I gave her my reactions as to whether the new part made her face look fuller or less full than before, whether it made her look younger or older, and how the change influenced her other features—"It shows your nice broad forehead"—so that together we related and communicated about her valuing of how she looked. It was obvious I shared her concern and wanted her to feel good about herself.

Often when I say something very positive to one of my children, I receive a reply like, "You only say that because you're my mother and mothers have to like their children." At that point, I might honestly admit I'm probably prejudiced in her favor because I'm her mother and I think she's terrific, but I'd go on to elaborate why I made the positive statement.

Our educational system with all its tests and evaluations is often not helpful to building self-esteem in children. The testing system is set up to highlight negative evaluations, since what gets marked and noticed are the wrong answers. Children are not getting validated for what they do correctly, which would nurture positive success, but evaluated in light of their failures. Often, not until college, and then only in certain courses, do teachers tend to write positive comments on test papers saying what was noticed and liked.

In building success in a relationship with children, there is a reciprocity involved. The adults benefit, too. Your value to the child is experienced, and your self-esteem is enhanced as you watch the successful effect of your esteeming the child. It's like the joy of watching your plants grow as you nurture and care for them.

Self-Esteem Principle: Nurturing success, the food of high self-esteem, comes from acknowledging the positive in a nonevaluative way.

20 ★ Acknowledge Children's Signs of Care

When children send you letters, bring you small gifts, show you something they've made, dress or wear something especially for you, or demonstrate any other sign of care and affection, acknowledge it in some way. It is a clear signal of a child's reaching out to establish a deeper bond in the relationship, and you can acknowledge their sign as a successful effort.

Angela, a second grader ostensibly sent to me for tutoring, was in reality considered a problem child by her teacher and described as being "bossy, selfish, uncooperative, and given to tantrums." During the year I worked with Angela, I don't think I ever experienced any of those qualities. In fact, it was often quite the opposite.

In my tutoring work with Angela, I began as I did with many children by having her draw a picture, give it a title, then write a sentence describing the picture. The direction of our work together involved going from a single sentence to a paragraph and then to a story filling a page or more. Our tutoring was focused on reading, writing, and comprehension. Not only did Angela cooperate in the process, but very soon she began bringing to our sessions booklets, fully gift-wrapped, ribboned, and addressed to me, with a picture drawn by her on the front and a title and story inside. She'd created the booklet idea and done the wrapping all by herself.

I was obviously being given a gift of what she thought I cared about most in our tutoring relationship. It's almost as if she had assigned herself homework and brought it to me as a gift! I was deeply touched by the care with which she wrapped and addressed the booklets as gifts, and said so. I esteemed her effort, her learning, her creativity, her generosity, and the thoughtfulness that went into all of it. I also found ways to acknowledge those qualities in her again and again throughout our work together.

Angela's penchant for bossiness also found its own successful, creative channel. After she felt comfortable with me, she would bring some of her classmates to my office during lunchbreak and lead them in short dramatic productions of her own creation, which all of us enjoyed. I was a captive yet appreciative audience. After performances, I rewarded everyone from a bag of treats which I kept in my desk for just such occasions. Angela was able to channel her bossy energy into a kind of leadership quality by organizing, producing, and directing her little dramas.

It's important to note here that Angela's peer relationships had been considered very poor before we began working together. Her teacher had warned me that not only did all her classmates dislike her, but some of them had even been sending her "hate notes." Considering second graders are not all that advanced in the skill of writing, hate notes seemed quite exceptional. Also exceptional was Angela's improvement in peer relationships as demonstrated in her recent noon-hour dramatic productions.

Angela's most extraordinary production involved at least six of her newly made friends in a surprise birthday party for me, complete with a ruse to get me out of my office for ten minutes (ostensibly to look at class artwork) while others hurriedly decorated my office with crepe paper, laid out colorful paper plates, napkins, cookies, candy, nuts, and even juice, and wrote "Happy Birthday" on the chalkboard. Angela had orchestrated the entire event down to assigning each child what to do and what to bring. They sang "Happy Birthday" as I entered the room and was truly surprised. On that day everyone's self-esteem increased, not the least my own.

You may be curious how Angela managed to gain the willing cooperation of her classmates who, just a few months before, had been reputed to dislike her so intensely. What had happened was very interesting. In tutoring, Angela and I agreed that for every sentence she correctly read or question she correctly answered, I would give her one Red Hot (a tiny cinnamon candy). This was a standard behavior-modification positive reinforcement technique I had used with students many times. However, Angela responded differently. Most children would pop the candy into their mouth as soon as I handed it to them. Angela saved hers. During a session, she carefully kept track of the number of candies she had earned; at the end of a session she carefully counted them out for herself from my supply and took them with her in a small plastic bag.

I had wondered what Angela did with that candy, but never asked. (I never thought to ask.) It was her teacher who enlightened me. My guess had been she ate them by herself at recess or took them home to show her mother her reward for a successful tutoring session. Something traditional like that. What she really had done was use my behavior-modification system on her classmates. Some might want to call it bribing, others like myself prefer to call it positive reinforcement. In any case, children who talked with Angela received candy, children who sat with her at lunch received candy, and children who invited her into their games received candy. I don't know if she herself ever ate any of those candies, but she did use them effectively to open the way for her classmates to learn to relate to her successfully. It was not unlike the way I had opened the door to her relating to me.

These were the children Angela invited to meet me. Over a period of time during lunchbreaks, she introduced me to a variety of classmates, who experienced my interest in them and also my treats. These were the children who enjoyed acting in Angela's plays and who were a part of my surprise birthday party. Angela had rewarded her friends not only with candy, but also with the opportunity to relate to me.

Angela seemed content with my showing interest in and care for her classmates. I wanted to know their names and anything else about themselves they were willing to tell me. Whenever I asked one of my "list of favorites" questions, we'd have a lively discussion. The old "bossy and selfish" Angela seemed quite content to be a part of the entire group's enjoyment.

One reason I never witnessed Angela's tantrums, another behavior she had been notorious for, was that I never allowed for them. Although I nurtured her creativity, I also kept very close watch over what happened during the time we spent together. I knew Angela's energies continually needed to be channeled in positive ways. For example, I noticed when Angela began to feel insecure, like the times when she was afraid she couldn't do something I requested of her, she would begin to grow angry and rebellious. Insecure people often mask their insecurity with anger. At such moments, I would stop the process and shift gears rather than force her forward in the initial direction. I would usually redesign the task, eliciting her cooperation and suggestions, in such a way that she could succeed. Thus, if with a tone of anger she said, "I can't do that. I don't want to do that," I might say, "Let's see if there's some way you could do it that would be more fun, that you wouldn't mind doing so much. What could we do?"

Providing a success-oriented structure was important for a child like Angela, who had much energy and many talents. I needed the cooperation of her mother and teacher in order to help reverse the negative self-image and negative behavior that seemed to be blocking her. This is not to say Angela became the ideal child. What we were able to do was identify the cycle of behavior destructive to her self-esteem and reverse it into a cycle that nurtured self-esteem.

Angela's deep desire to relate and be accepted was effectively shown in her wish to gift me and her classmates with signs of caring and affection. Her caring became a gateway to new levels of self-esteem and acceptance by others.

Self-Esteem Principle: Small tokens of care and affection are signs of a child reaching out in a relationship and of growing self-esteem.

21 ★ Capitalize on Existing Successes

In building success into a relationship with children, take advantage of what they already have going for them. Utilize the interests and successes that already exist. Find some way to make a child feel successful, then build more success upon that success.

When Tommy came to me, he experienced at least some satisfaction in drawing pictures, even if it wasn't clearly an example of success in the teacher's eyes. It's also likely he received acknowledgment from his family or others regarding his drawings. When he had drawn a picture and given me a story to go with it and experienced my valuing it, he possessed a clear understanding of one way he could be successful in our tutoring work together. First, the drawings and stories seemed productive to the academic learning experience we were about, so he knew success there. Second, the drawings and stories were predictably successful in earning esteem from me.

Earlier in talking about building success, I suggested capitalizing on a child's interests. The present approach, capitalizing on a child's existing success, takes us a step further. When interest has produced success, reinvest both the interest and success, thereby expanding the result to new interests and further successes. For example, Jimmy's interest in toys, which we discovered in looking at the Sears catalogue, allowed him to develop success not only in reading and writing, but also in organizational skills. From the Sears catalogue, Jimmy began keeping a notebook of toys, their descriptions, and prices. This investment of interest blossomed into an interest in cataloguing. Soon Jimmy began keeping records and notes (what scientists call research) about different kinds of things he found in nature. Interests and successes expanded again when Jimmy began a plant collection, which he kept neatly catalogued. In collecting and cataloguing plants he found around the school and at home, he developed an interest in ecology.

One day when I brought two crickets to class, we held a jumping contest. With a tape measure, we measured the largest jumps. The tape measure opened doors to new interests. We measured rooms, tables, desks, books, even ourselves. All of these measurements Jimmy kept dutifully in his record book. Reading and writing were learned very naturally and easily within this atmosphere of excited interest and successes.

Angela is an example of a girl who reinvested her successes with very little suggestion from me. From success in producing drawings and stories at my request, she went on to produce further stories and drawings at home, continuing her sense of accomplishment and reinforcing her feeling of success. Her success in friendships with classmates followed a similar growth pattern. At the first lunchbreak dramatic production, Angela had enlisted the help of two friends; by the time of my birthday party, she could count on at least six. Success here allowed her to deepen some relationships and to learn to handle complex relational arrangements with as many as six children. My delight and interest in her friends renewed her interest in making friends and exploring a network of relationships.

The story of Jimmy's expansion of academic interests was paralleled by Angela's expansion of social and relational interests. Each of them expanded their successes in both social and academic areas. As academic success developed for Jimmy, social success began to appear in his life as well. Angela moved from social success to academic success.

Another thing I often did to multiply success was to suggest the children show their accomplishments to their parents. Here, I insured parents' successful recognition of them as much as possible, thereby increasing the child's sense of success and self-esteem. Usually I would send a note home to parents with the child. For example, I might choose one of Tommy's pictures and stories and ask him to please show it to his family. On a piece of paper, I might write to his parents: "This is a delightful story. Tommy's creativity is really special, and I enjoy working with him."

Whenever I wrote a note like this, I would read it to the child. Then I left the envelope unsealed so the child could show the note to anyone he or she chose to. I worded my notes so parents would have a clear indication of where they might focus their acknowledgment of the child's success.

Self-Esteem Principle: Success builds most easily and most effectively on past successes. Success is most likely to be believed possible by children where they have had a history of similar successes.

22 ★ Watch for Growth Sparks

You will need to listen and watch carefully to catch a spark of interest when it happens. These are the sparks from which you can ignite the fire that motivates a child's personal growth in learning and in relationships.

Tommy provides a good example of catching a growth spark. When I began working with him, he was quite unaware of the world around him. He hadn't even noticed there was a railroad trestle outside my office window, when I happened to point it out to him after several tutoring sessions. I hoped I could get Tommy interested in learning about the world he lived in, as a way of getting him interested in learning in general. It occurred to me to take him outdoors and examine things. We started with the railroad trestle, then moved on to the plants and trees. We looked at the rings on felled trees and examined a few kinds of moss growing behind the building. So far, nothing seemed to excite him. But a spark of interest showed when we began comparing rocks. Rocks were things he could pick up, hold in his hand, put in his pocket and keep.

So we brought the rocks inside and put them on the windowsill. We pointed out some of their differences. Together we looked for rocks again. Next, I began bringing rocks to Tommy, saying, "I found this one in my backyard, this one on the street, and this one at the park." Soon Tommy began bringing rocks to show me and telling me where he'd found them. By now we had accumulated boxes of rocks. We glued each rock to a piece of cardboard and labeled where it came from.

There is an interesting aspect to Tommy's story. In my understanding of Jungian psychology and symbolism, rocks represent the self. It was my theory Tommy was symbolically taking hold, in his hands, of more and more parts of himself as he grew more aware of himself and of the world in which he lived. I felt the truth of my insight, especially when he would come to a tutoring session after some kind of negative experience in class or on the playground. At anxious times like these, he would ask before we began our academic work if we could go outside and "find rocks." When we did, I could watch him grow less anxious and more in touch with himself. Usually after a short time of finding rocks, he or I would indicate it was time to go inside and begin the tutoring work. Tommy seemed to have found a way to reassemble his broken self-esteem by doing (and sharing) something that felt familiar, satisfying, and successful, like collecting rocks.

I not only acknowledged his spark of interest by bringing him rocks I found, but also fanned it by talking about the rocks and giving them to him. Moreover, we lined them up on the windowsill in clear view of everyone who came into my room. It was very natural, then, for him to begin bringing in his own findings and to proudly add them to the rocks on the windowsill.

Comparing rocks, labeling them, boxing them were all sparks of interest. Each spark kept us building on our interest. As our rock collecting became more and more complex, our relationship deepened and grew more complex. We were present to each other at times outside the tutoring sessions, indicated by the rocks we brought to share. Whereas Tommy had given up on the world, seeing it as a place that was neither interested in him nor in which he was interested (knowing the details of Tommy's psychological history, I could understand why he had given up), rocks and an interest around rocks sparked a growing relationship of him with me and with the larger world.

In a similar way, I had been looking for a spark of interest to build on for Chuck in order to find reading material sufficiently motivating for him to want to work hard enough to get past the poor reading habits he had developed. Chuck was a learning-disabled child who skipped words and lines, who transposed words, and who had difficulty comprehending what he read. Children like Chuck with low self-esteem are often convinced they cannot grow, learn, or relate successfully.

I recognized a spark when Chuck came in one day and wanted to show me a magic trick he'd learned. I asked him where he learned it. He said, "It was on a cereal box." He enjoyed showing the trick to me, a clear sign of his interest, and he was glad about my delight in it. His self-esteem was clearly involved in my delight and interest in his trick.

With the spark present, what I did was go through all my children's books at home to see what I could find on magic tricks. I seemed to remember someone had given a book of magic tricks to one of my children. I found the book abandoned under my youngest daughter's bed.

I took the magic book to the next session, plus the items that would allow us to try the first trick—a glass, a coin, and a napkin, as I recall. Together we read the directions, and he practiced the trick until, to both our delight, he had mastered it.

Once the spark of interest had ignited, magic tricks evolved into scientific experiments. We began looking for experimental and technical books that were at a level he could master. When we found experiments to perform, he would willingly copy pages of instructions from a book. I also encouraged him to take what he had learned to show his family and friends.

From Chuck's spark of interest in magic and science, he experienced himself growing in learning. He was able to relate to me and others with the very skills he was developing. In all these ways he was growing in self-esteem. He began experiencing himself as a learning, growing, relating person.

Self-Esteem Principle: Children with low self-esteem tend to believe they can't grow, learn, or relate successfully.

23 ★ Keep a Record of Your Relationship

This principle focuses on the growth of a relationship between a child and an adult; the following principle emphasizes the child's growth in proficiency and skill. The tangible record of a relationship is important, especially at times when children are depressed and their low self-esteem tries to convince them they are not lovable or worth relating to. At times likes these, it is comforting and reassuring to return to some tangible record of how the relationship has survived and grown through difficult times. A concrete record helps affirm there were successes and there probably will be more.

For example, I keep all the letters my children have sent to me; these include postcards from camp, notes at holiday times, and now letters from college. Each child has a box with her name on it. In it I also keep their creative writing, starting with their earliest examples. I have much larger boxes to hold a lot of their drawings, most of which I have dated. I also keep their report cards, though for some children that might be embarrassing. My children enjoy going back in time while looking through these boxes. Each time they do, it seems to rekindle a bond between us.

Tommy's accumulating boxes of rocks and labels were a testimony to the amount of work and time we had spent together and the relating that went on.

When I worked as a diagnostic tutor and therapist, I made periodic written reports of my child-clients, which I also shared with them as a testimony of our relationship. In these reports,

I described their academic growth in terms they could understand, and I also described the process of learning, how we got from one step to the next. So the report was not merely a statement that the child had improved; it was a concrete description, with examples, of the evolution of our relationship and the child's learning from the beginning. Anyone who read the report could follow the process of our relationship and the learning steps, and experience some of the unique moments and variety in its history.

Sharing my reports with the children became almost a reliving of our growth together. We both could participate in the self-esteem it produced because we had participated in the reciprocal struggle involved in the growth.

Self-Esteem Principle: Children who are low self-esteemers often forget the growth, length, and depth of a relationship, especially at times when they feel insecure, depressed, fearful, or very needy.

24 ★ Point Out a Child's Increasing Skill

It is important to children's self-esteem that they know they are not only lovable but also capable. They are valued not only because they are relating children, but also because they can create and do things.

For the children I worked with in tutoring and counseling, I would keep a collection of their writings and drawings, with dates. With some children, I used artwork as an ongoing measure of their academic development. It seemed to me to be a measure of improvement that they could naturally grasp. I could say, "Look how you draw trees now, see all the leaves you add. Now look, when you first started drawing trees, they were smaller and not as filled with leaves. Look there, you even put birds in your trees now."

Or to another I might say, "Look at how many pictures

you've done in the past few months." When I worked with Hilda, she did one drawing per session, and I covered one of my office walls with her drawings arranged in chronological order. In this way, each time she came into my room, her growth history greeted her eyes. It was very easy to point out her increasing proficiency. "Look at all the details you're noticing and adding to your pictures now. See, this little girl you just drew even has shoelaces and a ribbon in her hair."

Children didn't just have to take my word they had grown. I could point it out to them in their own work. "See how your handwriting has improved."

When I worked with children in spelling, I kept notebooks of all the words they had learned. Whenever a child began to lose heart at the latest list of new words for spelling, I could show them the pages of words in my notebook which they had already mastered.

At home, like lots of parents, I used the refrigerator door and kitchen cabinets to display children's artwork or other things they had done. These surfaces, available for the whole family to see, kept at least the current part of the history of successful growth and accomplishments before our eyes.

Self-Esteem Principle: Evidence of success that is concrete— visible and tangible—has a strong positive effect on a child's self-esteem.

25 ★ Have No Unspoken Expectations

Expectations can sometimes evoke energy and excitement when you and the child share them openly and willingly. On the other hand, expectations can be a source of confusion and anxiety in children when they remain unstated or presumed. Furthermore, expectations, stated or unstated, often get in the way of certain kinds of creative success in children.

I find it helpful to distinguish between a task and an expectation. A task usually refers to what is to be accomplished. An expectation usually refers primarily to the where, when, and how by which a task is carried out. While it is important that you and the child clearly understand and agree upon the task, it is also important to realize that both you and the child may differ in your expectations (usually unspoken) of how, when, and where the task is to be done. So in building success into your relationship with a child, I would tend to allow for the child's when, where, and how to guide the way the task is carried out.

Fourteen-year-old Kerry was working on our School Readiness Program team, getting preschoolers in a small, poor Southern town ready for their first-grade experience. I assigned Kerry the task of taking a group of five children aside to work with them on counting skills. I didn't tell her how or where to do her task, but I did expect she would take the children to one of the tables in the back of the room and use the blocks and rods there to teach counting.

Ten minutes later, I was surprised to notice that Kerry and the children weren't at the back tables, so I went looking for them. I found them in the entrance hall. (We were using a church for our schoolhouse.) She was teaching them to count by having them jump up and down the stairs, so their entire bodies were involved in the counting. Another technique she used, as I watched unnoticed, was having children push chairs across the floor from one side of the hall to the other; the child would say "one" for the first chair pushed, "two" for the second chair, and so on. This form of counting was another total-body experience. Kerry had found two whole-body techniques for teaching counting I would never have thought of. Her methods came out of her own creative response to my request. I had assigned the task, she had found a successful way of carrying it out. Her sense of herself being able to carry out a task using her own creative resources increased her own self-esteem.

If I had made my original expectations known ("Here's the

way I'd do it, Kerry, if I were you."), she probably would have carried them out my way; but we would have missed an excellent opportunity for her imagination to be exercised and for a new learning technique to be discovered.

While some insecure young people might have been threatened when I did not show them how to carry out the task, Kerry was not threatened, and I knew that. I also knew she felt secure in her capacity to teach. If she felt she needed guidance, she would have asked for it. Her expectation on that score was clear: she knew she could get guidance from me. What this approach opens up is a way of facilitating a success that Kerry, or any young person in similar circumstances, could own totally.

Sometimes adults get caught presuming, because they've done things successfully a certain way in the past, "That's the way it should be done," or "That's always the best way," and "If only children would cooperate they'd realize that's the best way for them to learn, too." For me, at times like this, it's as if an inner expectation messenger tells me, "Children will certainly learn counting best when I teach them my way. My way works." When I'm in this closed mood, I find I am apt to ignore suggestions from the students that other ways be tried, and I am tempted to cut them off by saying, "Do it my way," or "Do it the way I told you."

On the other hand, when I explore the possibility of using some new, alternative ways (which are not necessarily better, but different), particularly if the suggestions come from children themselves, I am opened to a new level of involvement with them. I can begin then to value and esteem their involvement in their own learning, their willingness to contribute to the *how* of the task.

Self-Esteem Principle: Avoid having rigid expectations and demands on how and when a task is to be carried out by a child when you're trying to build that child's sense of success.

26 ★ Keep Expectations Realistic

Have certain expectations if you must (and you probably must), but let them be reasonable and practical for the children you deal with. What seems reasonable to you may not be so for them. To have expectations that are too high for them promotes failure rather than success.

One expectation I had of my children was they would clean their rooms each weekend. I didn't feel it was an unrealistic expectation, and I expressed it very clearly: it was an open-ended expectation that they have their rooms neat and clean by Sunday night; they were free to do the cleanup any time over the weekend, as long as it was completed by Sunday night. I felt the expectation was practical, reasonable, and easy to live up to.

However, over and over again Sunday night came and their rooms remained uncleaned. I grew frustrated, and found myself not only nagging at them but also threatening. "If your room isn't cleaned up before you go to bed tonight," I would say on a Sunday night, "no television next week." So late at night I would have a tired and grumbling daughter cleaning her room, and I knew I was going to have an even more tired and grumbling daughter next morning.

Several unsuccessful ploys were tried by my daughters. The first was hiding everything in the closet. When I complained about the closet, things got shoved under the bed. I found my role changing from a parent who was asking for some cooperation in keeping the house clean to a parent who was snooping in the children's rooms to see how well they'd done the task or how well they succeeded in avoiding it. Somehow on this point the sense of cooperation among us got lost.

My growing frustration and anger exploded when one of my daughters cleaned up her room by putting all her freshly laundered clothes (left on her bed waiting to be put into drawers or hung in the closet by her) into the clothes hamper with all her dirty laundry. When I found myself doing her clean laundry all over again, I realized she and I had moved from a lack of cooperation into an adversary situation.

I never did find any satisfactory solution for getting rooms cleaned. We settled for some compromises, which seemed to be the way things remained. I treated their rooms as their space and their responsibility. I still complained at times that their rooms looked like they had stirred them with a big stick. Once, I asked them if they could easily spend so many hours talking on the phone, couldn't they spend even a little time cleaning their rooms with the same energy? Their answer was clearly "no." I guess I realized that even for myself, thinking about housecleaning did not generate the same enthusiasm as the thought of talking on the phone with a friend.

Perhaps I might have been more successful (I like to succeed, too!) if from the beginning I could have accepted room cleaning on their terms. I realize now my expectation was they would clean their rooms the way I wanted them cleaned, that is—no clothing stuffed and unhung, things put in their place, etc. Clearly, my expectations were too high for them.

In discussing problems with some adults at a workshop on the family, a number of them expressed feeling their own parents had had expectations of them they felt were unreasonable. Yet the unreasonableness had never been discussed or confronted.

When expectations are necessary, it helps if they are as clearly defined as possible, discussed and understood by everyone concerned, and open to reexamination from time to time. Most of all, they need to be realistically appropriate to that unique child at a particular time. (I am surprised to note that my daughters in college now have a reputation for having clean and neat rooms. I can't explain their change.)

I want to make a special note about the children I characterize as *pleasers*. These are children who will do (or agree to do) anything they think will please you. When you ask them to do something, they usually respond with an immediate yes without taking the time to think about whether they really want to do it. Often enough they find themselves doing something they resent. An adult who is unaware of the pleaser's dynamics usually won't be able to figure out why this child (a pleaser) is giving them a hard time, since only a short time ago the very same child had said, "That's what I want to do." Often the pleaser-child can't figure out why they're resenting it either. The reason is that they never got in touch with whether they really wanted to do it in the first place; their perception of wanting or not wanting was short-circuited by their overwhelming need to please.

I am familiar with this dynamic because I tend to be a pleaser myself. I need to be aware that in my own wish to be a pleaser I am tempted to use my own children as surrogates. For example, even though I know my children do not enjoy baby-sitting, I have caught myself wanting to please the neighbors by volunteering my daughters to baby-sit. "You'd like to baby-sit for the Greens, wouldn't you?" I have heard myself saying; or worse, "I told Mrs. Green you'd love to baby-sit for her." Things like this really confuse a child, especially when the child finds herself becoming infected by the pleaser mentality.

Aside from having pleaser parents, some children have parents who offer no behavioral guidelines or structure. Everything seems acceptable and no boundaries are set, at least not openly. But beneath it all are unexpressed expectations. When children don't live up to these unexpressed expectations, they get scolded. Never clearly knowing what's expected, what's forbidden, or what's acceptable begins to make children feel insecure. Consequently, they live in constant fear of accidentally violating one of the unstated and unknown rules. Such children sense there are expectations present in the adult's mind, but don't know what they are. Alll this can lead a child to become super-sensitive and extremely self-critical.

Self-Esteem Principle: Low self-esteem children often feel anxious to please others. Clearly stating your expectations will help them feel less anxious.

27 ★ Be Aware You Are a Model

During times you are together with your children, share yourself fully but without overwhelming them. Let yourself respond honestly to the experiences that happen to you. For your children, you are a model of who they can become, so they will need to see this model in action and will watch you very closely. Use your opportunities to model for them healthy ways of being and relating in the world.

I remember accompanying Miranda to the jewelry store after Christmas to exchange an expensive wristwatch for a watch more appropriate to her daily needs. With the help of the store owner, she selected another watch. As they were finishing their financial transactions, I realized the owner had overcharged us, and I called it to his attention. When he denied it, I responded quietly but assertively, without getting angry or backing down and apologizing. I simply said, "I wish you would check your figures again, for the figures as I understand them are different from yours." Politely but firmly, I made it clear the transaction would go no further until my request was responded to. It turned out I had been correct. When the shopkeeper apologized and made the necessary adjustments on our receipt, I simply said, "I understand. Thank you."

When Miranda and I stepped outside the shop, she said she was really glad I'd stood up for her because she wouldn't have known how to do it. She felt she would have just simply accepted his word and left, while feeling confused and probably angry at herself for allowing herself to be ripped off. She affirmed my modeling, saying she felt what I had done was to be firm but not insulting, and I had found a way for the issue to be cleared up so that nobody felt badly in the end. Nobody lost any self-esteem.

A similar occurrence happened to another of my children when a salesclerk was rude to her. I returned with my daughter to the store, stated to the salesclerk I was displeased with the way my daughter had been treated, and said I felt the clerk's attitude was unacceptable. My daughter learned she did not have to accept treatment of her that diminished her self-esteem. "No matter what age you are," I explained to my daughter, "you have a right to respect and consideration, and you can make your feelings known when you feel hurt by other people's devaluing of you." I modeled for her a way to be assertive of my rights and of her rights on her behalf.

I've found the best way to be assertive is to do it briefly, directly and without anger, but to do it very clearly, including a statement of my feelings. Being assertive does not come easy to me. I don't like confrontations, and my daughters know that. The two encounters with salespeople I just told about were acts of considerable bravery as far as I'm concerned. But I think it was important for my daughters (and for me, too) that I stretched myself a bit for them to see me that way, so they could learn from it for themselves.

While I might have done these acts of assertiveness primarily for my daughters' sake, I also enhanced my own sense of self as a person capable of responsible confrontation, and in touch with and articulate about my feelings and needs.

Dealing with personal needs and wants is an area where children require models. Given our cultural values, it is often very difficult for adults to express their own wants and needs without somehow feeling selfish. Yet it is very important for children to see in their adult models persons who care for themselves appropriately by acknowledging their needs and wants in the world, persons who are willing to put energy into asserting themselves for these ends while also being at times willing to compromise, postpone, and even sacrifice these wants and needs, but doing so by conscious choice. When foregoing one's wants is done consciously and reasonably, self-esteem is enhanced, not diminished. In contrast, consider the

parents who seldom take time for themselves and who are always willing to give up their own plans on behalf of their children. While children may enjoy having mom and dad at their
beck and call, another message comes across: to be an adult
means to have no needs or wants other than those of your children.

A healthier response to children's requests is to see if, together, parents and children can come up with an alternative
that allows both children and parents to keep their own plans.
I'm thinking of times my children volunteered me to drive a
carload of friends to a soccer game or a party when I had made
other plans. Instead of canceling my plans, I might suggest an
alternative: "Instead of me driving you and staying through the
game, what if I drop you off at the game; can you find someone
else to bring you home?" Usually, they could.

When I was in the throes of graduate school, my children
wanted time on the weekends to do fun things with friends,
while I needed many hours for study. I discovered I could take
them to the university swimming pool (even together with a
few friends), and leave them to play in the water while I stud-
ied my books on the sidelines. In that way, I remained present
and available to them while I took care of my needs and they
of theirs. They could see I valued my own needs as well as
theirs and had discovered an alternative acceptable to all of
us.

I feel one of the most important skills adults can model for
children is the flexibility to think creatively in order to find
alternative solutions to problems: finding creative ways to meet
your own needs and those of your children. We naturally feel
better when our needs are being met and when we know that
others' needs are being met as well. In a successful context like
this, self-esteem grows.

Self-Esteem Principle: Children with low self-esteem often
need a model for responding to experience, and they may look
to you to show the way a high self-esteemer might respond.

28 ★ Don't Bore Children

If you know something bores children, don't do it unless you have to. And if you have to, try to find a way of doing it that's less boring. The idea is that some things which need to be done in life are going to appear to be boring, at least when first encountered. The challenge is for you and the child together to find some way of relieving the boredom. For example, in spelling.

Spelling is very boring for a lot of children, but with some creative energy there are ways to make it less so. Here are some innovative ways of practicing spelling my tutoring children and I have thought of.

One child admired cheerleaders, so we turned spelling words into doing cheers, and she was able to chant the letters in a loud voice and devise different body movements for each letter. Pedagogically, this was an excellent technique, for her whole body was involved in the learning, and she began to respond with gusto to what she expected would be nothing but a boring task.

With Sandy we settled for a tracing method of learning to spell. We had a preliminary discussion about how tracing letters would get boring, and we both regretted that. "But at least we know how long the boring time will last," I said, "and you can set our timer and stop when it rings." In that way, we made the task containable with clear time boundaries. We also agreed to follow our spelling period with a more enjoyable task, like drawing. We utilized these rewards to make a boring task more tolerable.

One child suggested a way of humorously dealing with each spelling word by requiring, when a word was given or spelled on the board, that we create a silly sentence that included the spelling word. No restrictions were placed on the silly sentence, such as it had to make sense or be appropriate for a classroom.

Another activity commonly boring to children is a long ride in a car. Here, caring parents will want to prepare by taking along games to pass the time or suggesting car games. The point is that children are not left to the teasing and bickering that naturally sprout up among them when they grow bored. If children themselves help select games before a trip and the drive is enjoyed by all, the children feel cooperative and valuable, and their self-esteem will grow.

In general, if there's a boring task that must be done with children and there are no avoidances or alternatives, try to involve the children in the acceptance of the task and the responsibility to do it as enjoyably as possible. This involvement is likely to affect a child's self-esteem positively.

What you say about a boring activity is also important. First of all, acknowledge the child's likely feeling by saying, "I understand this is not your favorite activity. I know it's something you'd rather not have to do." Children's self-esteem is involved in having their authentic feelings accepted and acknowledged. In fact, when children's feelings are acknowledged, they often become less resistant to the task that aroused those feelings. I'm thinking, for example, of Teddy, who dropped most of his resistance to reading, spelling, and comprehension when he discovered he could help design and schedule the learning tasks.

It's helpful if children know you also *value* their feelings of boredom and resistance. One way to do this is not to deny them. Another way is to agree to cooperate with them in minimizing the negative or boring aspects of a task. Third, if a child, like Sandy, knows exactly how long they must tolerate a task, they might be more willing to accept the boredom if it's seen as something finite.

As a tutor, I continually faced the challenge of finding interesting material to keep sessions from being boring. That's one of the reasons I asked my "list of favorites" questions early on. They were not just idle questions to relax the children, but their responses gave me hints of how to keep the tutoring from being a bore. I didn't keep my researching a secret from the children, either, but explained how I had chosen this or that material for them because I thought they were interested in it. They knew I didn't want their sessions to be boring. When teaching reading, for example, if a child said the material was boring, I accepted that, and together we searched for alternative reading materials.

I am not trying to develop children who are unable to tolerate boredom and frustrations. Often the children and I explicitly discussed the fact that certain things in life are going to be boring and less interesting than other things. My real emphasis was in helping them cope with boredom and frustration creatively. I wanted to help develop flexible, imaginative children who will know how to seek alternative solutions to the problems they will face in life. In short, I wanted to prepare them for sucess, and to give them a sense of themselves as being capable of living successful lives.

This did not mean they would be able to live life just on their own terms. They knew that already, all too well. Instead of simply resigning ourselves to being helpless, we looked for creative alternatives. We looked for ways to put our lives in harmony with the world, to match our growth with its demands. Self-esteem is heightened not only by continuing successes, but also by children feeling a sense of involvement and control in their own life process as it joins the larger world.

Self-Esteem Principle: Boredom depresses esteem; interest and excitement increase the sense of self; an active involvement in life nourishes self-esteem.

IV

Bridging to a Loving World

People build bridges in order to go from one place to another, sometimes to a previously inaccessible place. Bridging to a loving world means establishing healthy connections between your children and the people, places, and situations that make up their loving world. Without such a bridge, made possible by you, children, especially those with low self-esteem, are apt to see much of the larger world not as loving and inviting, but hostile and menacing.

As a bridge builder, your task is first to connect children with who they are now and where they stand now—on one side of the bridge. Next, show them what they can reasonably expect to find on the other side. Then, offer them invitations to step across into this larger world and discover friendship and support, to relate and to care, to feel alive and to develop realistic trust and healthy skepticism.

I say healthy skepticism because things in the larger world are not to be trusted indiscriminately. Carefully select pieces of the larger world which represent its loving potential and connect children with these first, so they're motivated to want to explore further. Help them feel safe, at least in certain parts of the larger world.

I believe self-esteem will grow more rapidly when it is built on success and when it is in anticipation of joining the more attractive parts of the larger world. In turn, healthy self-confidence in children usually helps them discriminate the safe from the unsafe, the desirable from the undesirable in the larger world. As help, I teach them to trust their own emotions and talents and to view these in the context of the larger world.

Building bridges involves giving a lot of yourself to your children.

29 ★ Invest Something of Yourself in the Child

Let children be involved with you in something outside the ordinary, programmed situation. Let them know you are willing to invest something personal of yours in your relationship with them.

While I was working to develop self-grooming in Hilda, at a very early developmental stage, I used to pick her up and hold her next to me in front of the mirror in my office. She was so little at five years old, weighing only twenty-eight pounds, I could easily hold her with my left arm.

It was winter cold outside, and we had both been wearing hats on our walk from the nursery school to the building where my office was. When we took our hats off, our hair was full of static electricity. As I lifted her up to look at ourselves in the mirror, I could see our hair needed combing. Spontaneously, I reached for a comb from my purse and began combing my hair. I then asked Hilda if she wanted her hair combed. She nodded a yes.

At first I began to comb her hair, but then I handed her the comb and let her comb her own hair. Then I invited her to comb mine.

I had done a simple act of bridging her to a new place of

self-grooming. She was repeating my actions, combing her hair, then mine.

As she was learning grooming, she was also relating to me as part of the larger world. Being held in my arms, she could physically feel the closeness of our relationship, and she could also see it by looking at our faces close together side by side in the mirror. Thus, another instance of bridging was happening.

Both these steps were tremendous milestones for Hilda, since she was known to be an untouchable and unrelating child. Her willingness to let me touch her and have her touch me was really an act of mutual investment.

This bridging was done nonverbally. A bridging to verbal relating would come in time. But for a child not used to responding at all, she had done well. The combing provided a focus that relieved her from directly confronting her fear of the physical closeness we were sharing.

The combing had a very special bridging quality. The fact it was my comb and not a child's comb or a toy added a special note of intimacy. I had to reach into *my purse* to get the comb. That comb was a piece of my intimate life, my personal grooming equipment. And I shared it with her.

Children at the school with whom I shared lunch also offered me an opportunity of investing something of myself. With Sharon in particular, part of our regular session was eating lunch together. In fact, with this 14-year-old girl I built entire therapy sessions around sharing lunch. She attended a school for retarded and emotionally disturbed children in the building next door. It seemed we needed some structure for our work together, because at fourteen she considered herself too old for play therapy. Her teachers reported a lot of resistance in her to academic subjects, so I didn't want to approach her directly through school work. Eating seemed to provide a time, a framework, and an activity we could comfortably share.

I brought things in my lunch like cookies and fruit which I

intended to share with her. "These bananas looked really good," I might say to Sharon, "and I thought we might enjoy eating a banana together today," or "My daughters made these cookies last night. I thought you'd like them, so I brought some for us."

The cookies were special because they provided bridges for Sharon to a number of places in the loving world: to my children, because they had made the cookies; to me, because I thought of her when I brought them; and to our relationship, because we both liked them and shared them. It was also a personal investment, because I felt free to bring things my children made to share with her; it was almost like sharing my children with her.

Self-Esteem Principle: When you share something of yourself with children, it increases their value of themselves and builds self-esteem.

30 ★ Tell Children They are Part of Your World

Whenever I brought something of my own children's world into my professional work, for example, when I used their suggestions, their toys, and their games, I made a point of building my children's self-esteem by telling them how useful their suggestions had been.

Children I worked with often taught me things I then used in working with others. Hilda, for example, did a drawing for me each session. Using a series of these drawings, I could clearly graph her ego growth. I wrote a report on her work and presented it at a staff meeting. They were very excited about drawing both as a diagnostic tool and as a therapeutic technique for ego growth. After the meeting, I told Hilda how impressed the staff was by her artwork and by the large number of pictures she had drawn. I told her they not only liked what she did, but some of them planned to use similar ideas in their own work with children. I would guess she felt good knowing something she did was liked by the larger world, could be useful to it, and helpful to other children.

Plants make good bridges. Chuck brought me grapefruit seeds he had planted and sprouted. I took them home to let them grow in my own home and kept Chuck informed of their progress. In this way, he knew something of his had a place in my home.

I brought a spider plant from home to my office. It was a plant Miranda had grown and given to me. She knew a part of her was with me in my office. Hilda used to water this spider plant when she came for her sessions. At holiday time, I let her take it home so she could have it with her and care for it. After vacation, she brought it back and continued to care for it. When her therapy was over, I gave the plant to her with Miranda's approval. That plant did a lot of bridging in its day.

It's an act of valuing them to bring something of children into your world, but it's even more special to their self-esteem when you give them feedback on what it means to you. My children could better tolerate my work as a therapist and my hours of being away from them because they knew they were among the resources I used, and I told them how they helped my professional work.

Self-Esteem Principle: Children's self-esteem grows when they know they are having a positive effect on the larger world.

31 ★ Utilize the Natural Environment

There were a number of children I worked with who, when they first came to me, had not been relating well to anything or anybody. I am thinking of Tommy, who never noticed a railroad trestle outside my window; Sharon, who didn't relate to people or to school; and Hilda, who was mute and almost immobile. Children who seem continually unaware of what they see and where they are need to establish a basic grounding in fundamental activity. This is usually done most effectively by helping them make a connection with their environment.

Other children become temporarily unrelating and out of touch when dealing with difficult emotional situations. The natural environment can also be helpful here. I am reminded of Chuck, who needed to deal with his anxiety about separation when he had come to our last tutoring-therapy session. The park became for us a neutral environment. We rested on the soft grass and enjoyed looking at cloud formations. It was a way of being connected that didn't make too many demands on us. Nature is nice that way. It's easy to relate to.

One of the things I did with Sharon and Hilda was pick flowers together in the spring. Both girls were frightened of people; they needed to learn to relate in positive ways and to communicate. It was important we find something we could both acknowledge as lovely, enjoyable, and familiar. Again, nature provided a way. We'd search through the grass for tiny wildflowers on the way from the school building to my office. Sometimes we'd just look at them, sometimes we'd pick a few and bring them inside.

Noticing was the activity in which we were really engaged. Noticing proved to be a nonthreatening way of relating. The day-care patients always grew a vegetable garden outside the clinic, which provided us with a good place to sit and notice things. I often used a ritual of noticing there with Sharon and Hilda. We probably spent more time watching the garden than the day-care patients did.

I tried to get Hilda to actively relate to nature, to touch and handle things. For example, I taught her how to blow dandelion puffs, something nobody had ever done with her. Sometimes she'd wave them in the air as if they were magic wands.

I also showed Hilda how to curl dandelion stems. "When you pick a dandelion with a long stem," I explained, "you can split it at the bottom so you get at least two sections. Then when you dip the ends in water, they curl up." I split and curled one to show her how, then let her try curling one.

One of the things happening in all this was we were looking at familiar things. Because they were natural and constant, they would always be available in the environment. In that, they represented a grounding in life. The earth represents a level of reality that is very concrete and simple. Whether or not you pay attention to it or come back to look at it, the grass will grow and the wild flowers will bloom.

Another reassuring thing about nature, as far as low-self-esteem children are concerned, seems to be its seasonal nature. This year's flowers are gone now, but they know next year there will be new flowers. I can show them how it's quite the same in their own lives. Some opportunities are gone now, I explain, but new opportunities will soon sprout up. This session is over now, but there'll be another session next week. Nature reminds us of this continuity.

Relating in therapy seemed a lot like growing a garden. Its lesson was process: we were always somewhere in process. Noticing nature taught children to trust nature's process, to let it move at its own pace, and not to rush it.

I sometimes found myself trying to get a child to do something they weren't yet ready to do. There have been any number of times I've found myself, like other parents and teachers, thinking this child was capable of doing something when they weren't really fully ready. I thought of the times my children begged me to get them a pet, promising to feed and care for it. I got them the big dog they wanted. But when the novelty of the dog wore off, what I prophesied turned out to be true, despite all their protestations to the contrary. The children no longer seemed interested in feeding it, walking it, and cleaning up after it.

I realized too late that my children's enthusiasm coincided with my wish that they were mature enough to accept responsibility for keeping a dog. However, both their enthusiasm and my wish had been unrealistic. A dog is a marvelous natural bridge to a loving world. Relating to a pet helps children learn about caring in a human relationship. But I had forgotten that learning to be responsible in a relationship (even with a dog) doesn't happen overnight, and enthusiasm alone cannot make up for lack of certain levels of maturity. It's not likely at the outset that young children can take complete care of a dog—feeding, brushing, walking, washing, cleaning up messes—but they can begin in one area, such as feeding.

It takes a certain amount of willpower to be helpful in developing responsibility in a child. It's probably easier to say, "Oh, I'll feed the dog when you go off to school." But it's so much more a gift to your child in the long run to help them enter successfully into the fundamental responsibility which allows them to say, "This is my dog, I feed it."

Don't expect total responsibility to happen quickly. It's a process that matures slowly.

There are moments in everyone's life where all you can do is something very simple, concrete, and manageable. And maybe that's enough for that moment.

Self-Esteem Principle: Whenever children's self-esteem begins to disappear and they find it difficult to relate to people and to working, start again by making simple concrete connections to the natural world.

32 ★ Let Children Share You with Others

You remember Angela, who shared with other children the cinnamon candies she earned during our sessions, who worked with her classmates on a surprise birthday party for me, and brought her friends to my office at lunch time for treats and drama? All of these activities are examples of how this principle works. I became Angela's special friend for her to share with her peers. It was almost as though I was seen as an extension of her. She had some control over who would be introduced to me and who among her classmates would be brought to my office.

When I sent notes home with children to be read by teachers and parents, it was as though they carried me back into their other worlds, and I could be an advocate there on their behalf. For example, when I sent notes home with Tommy describing to his parents how impressed I had been with his artwork, he could talk about me to his family and what I'd said about him, and how I had esteemed him in many positive ways. He could describe and feel the sense of value I gave him now augmented by the valuing his parents and others reflected back to him.

Sometimes children asked to take things of mine home with them. This happened with Harold, a four-year-old, highly disturbed boy attending the therapeutic nursery, who had problems with separation. He was an only child; both parents were elderly and had heart conditions. It's likely he sensed some of their fears about their health, and this brought up fears of loss and separation in him. He found it difficult to become an integral part of the school world, was extremely nonrelating, and would often hide from the other children under a table in the rear of the nursery.

Harold was more at ease in my office than in the nursery, since being in the office with me felt like home for a mother and child. While it was easy to get Harold to come to my office, he invariably resisted returning to the nursery. He would ask if he could take something from my office with him and bring it back next time he came.

The usual procedure, when such a request is made by a child in a therapeutic situation, is to say, "No. These toys belong here in this room. Other boys and girls come here and need to use them, too." With Harold I decided it was probably more important to emphasize a sense of continuity; as long as he left with a borrowed toy, he knew he would see me again. Psychologically, he carried with him, till the next therapy session, a concrete piece of our therapy room and his experience of me. Each time, then, I would let him choose some toy or item to take. He would usually share it with his classmates and show it to his family at home. He never failed to bring back what he had taken.

Psychologically, one could call such items *transition objects*. For Harold they created a bridge between the therapy room and other areas in his life. He invested, in such objects, the sense of success and self-esteem building he associated with the therapy room, and naturally, he wanted a way to carry that success around with him.

It's an interesting sidelight that Harold's parents offered to buy him toys just like the ones he brought home from my office. Harold would say no. He didn't want his own. Evidently the toys and items were valuable to him precisely because they belonged to me and my office space and weren't replaceable by others even if they looked the same. Though the toys were fun to play with, fun wasn't of primary importance for Harold. For him it was the connection, the bridging of one world into another.

It's interesting to note that when therapy was completed and Harold was able to attend a regular school on a regular basis, I asked him what he would like to take from my room to keep for his very own. He said, "Nothing, because the toys should stay here for other girls and boys to play with."

I think we both understood he no longer needed a toy to be his bridge. His own self-esteem had grown enough that he didn't need to carry a concrete object of mine to remind him of who he was with me. He had internalized that by now.

Self-Esteem Principle: Whatever gives a child a sense of control or personal worth helps self-esteem grow.

33 ★ Share Something That's Yours

Children like to touch and hold things, especially things that are associated with people special to them. As I mentioned before, I used to bring things to early therapy sessions I thought might interest the children—a prism, a kaleidoscope, a telescope, a magic box, a music box, a camera, a stamp collection, etc. Often these things belonged to my own children, and I might explain, for example, that the prism belonged to Wanda and was given to her by her cousin Michael. I might even add it had been a present for her tenth birthday; it had originally been Michael's prism, she had seen it at his home and liked it, and he gave it to her. The children in therapy could then share not only the object, but also some of its history and connection to members of my family.

It is also very special to let children hold and touch something you have worn. In this way, you are sharing with them something you have chosen for yourself. One favorite was a necklace, the pendant of which was a magnifying glass. I'd take it off and hand it to a child. With it they could examine their skin, fingernails, clothing, or anything else that occurred to them. I might tell them how this necklace had been given to me by a cousin who lived on a goat farm in Pennsylvania, a story that invariably raised questions. This magnifying-glass necklace often bridged difficult beginnings with a new child. Sometimes it even went overnight to some child's home.

I have a large carved bracelet given to me by a close friend who told me how it was made. When I showed the bracelet to children, I explained the process of how it was made and how it had been a special gift to me. I was also, thereby, indirectly presenting lessons in sharing gifts.

Intangible things facilitate relating, too, as long as they're things that speak of you. Sometimes I would tell my children in therapy jokes my own children brought home from school or from their friends. I might begin by saying, "This is a joke Miranda brought home from school."

Often I would get another joke in reply, sometimes with the request that I take it home and tell it to my children, an evident wish for bridging to a loving world. When my children responded to such a joke, I would report to the child at school, "I told my children your joke. They liked it and told their friends at school."

I began making a point of writing down such jokes. "I want to write this down so I don't forget it," I would honestly say. Not only did writing it down help me remember the joke, but it produced a whole set of self-esteem effects. It showed my students were important not only to me, but also to my children, and to their friends. They felt they had given me something of value.

I could be the bridge connecting my children in therapy with a larger world. The bridge could be crossed in both directions, passing information and objects, jokes and stories, reaching a world and being reached by a world they could not touch directly yet.

While some children need a bridge to their immediate, surrounding world, as Harold did to his nursery-school classmates, other children are ready to extend their reach to a much larger world.

Self-Esteem Principle: Children's self-esteem grows when they know that you want to share with them something you value, and that seems to them to be a part of you.

34 ★ Allow Children to be of Help to You

Letting children help you lets them get close to you. It is a concrete sign of your trust in them. When you acknowledge some of your needs to children and allow them to help you, it can provide a bridge for children to grow close to you and feel valued in your presence.

I've mentioned many times already how my own children were helpful to me in giving me toys, games, and ideas to use in my work with other children.

I remember preparing my tutoring lessons one evening, trying to figure out a way to help Sandy learn to do sequential work and discriminatory tasks. One technique I'd learned was to have a child practice sequencing and discriminating skills by going through a page of written material circling or underlining, for example, each letter *E* that appeared. The challenge was to be able to concentrate on marking the letters in the order they appeared.

Sandy had a problem using this technique, however. She got caught up in reading the text, and not looking for *E*'s. One of the reasons we were working at sequencing and discrimination was that she often transposed letters and words when she read stories. Rather than continuing to frustrate her by using this technique with intelligible words and sentences, I had come up with the idea of using a page of nonsense words to teach discrimination; I hoped this would keep the poor reading habits we were trying to correct from getting in our way. I typed out a page of nonsense words, ones she couldn't make any sense of, and my plan did succeed to a degree. But Sandy didn't really enjoy it, and I found it tedious and time-consuming to type out sheets full of nonsense words. But I kept doing it since it seemed the only way.

"Why are you typing that stuff, mom?" Wanda asked me, looking over my shoulder. "What are you doing?"

I explained to Wanda my dilemma, and how I was trying to solve Sandy's learning difficulty.

Wanda said, "I've got an idea," then disappeared. A few moments later she returned with a French magazine. Wanda was studying French at school, someone had donated a pile of French magazines to the school, and Wanda had inherited some of them. Wanda assured me the magazines were hers and she was free to give me one to mark up as much as I wanted to.

Sandy, who was ten at the time, was delighted with the French magazine and all its photos. Occasionally, amid all the French, an ad would appear with the brand name in English, which she enjoyed pointing out to me.

More importantly, the French magazine saved me from hours of work inventing pages of nonsense words. Sandy delighted in performing sequencing and discriminating skills on the unfamiliar French words. She even practiced at home.

In addition, Sandy's self-esteem was enhanced by having this special, foreign-language magazine. She knew it came from Wanda, who wanted her to have it.

Wanda, by the way, was proud of herself (and so was I) for having come up with such a clever idea. She knew she was helpful; she could enjoy the success. I also told her so and thanked her.

I've found it's been very helpful for me to tell children what I have learned from them. Instead of leaving my gratitude at a generalized level by saying, "I've learned a lot working with you," I like to go on to tell them in particular some of the learning moments that have happened between us, what they have meant to me, how I've been able to use their stories or ideas in working with other people, but especially what they have meant to me in terms of my own growth. For example, in a letter from college, Joan told me a way she'd found to deal with the times when she feels depressed, isolated, and non-valuable. Her idea was to find somebody she could do something for. "Instead of curling up into a cocoon of isolation," she wrote, "I force myself into some kind of action that helps me relate to others."

I found Joan's principle very helpful to me in my own life shortly after receiving her letter. Her wisdom helped me break out of a period of isolation and lethargy in my own life. I wrote to tell her how helpful she had been to me and how I had put her idea into practice.

Sometimes, even when people have a larger purpose in the world, like getting a degree or working for a cause, this larger purpose cannot counteract the occasional depression.

People need a specific concrete purpose for being alive during such times. Some simple action like a phone call to a friend or picking up a towel to dry dishes can often act as bridge from having no meaning in the world to having some meaning, at least for the moment.

Your self-esteem grows because you begin again to feel meaningful and useful; you can see the results of your productivity, and you may even be rewarded by a friend's "Thank you" for the favor you did.

Self-Esteem Principle: Children's self-esteem grows when they feel they can be genuinely helpful to you, or can help satisfy some of your needs. Be sure to give them feedback when they do.

35 ★ Act as a Bridge to the Outside World

You will remember how Tommy allowed me into his world by doing drawings and telling me stories about them. He was a student who had not been relating either to schoolwork or his classmates, and seemed to be interested only in drawing pictures. I entered his world in order to start building a bridge then. He helped me relate to him by telling me stories about his pictures. From his world, we went and looked at the larger world. Our first outing took us to the plants, trees, and rocks. We were able to establish an entire program of learning around collecting and cataloguing. From there we built bridges to more of the environment and finally to the people in his life.

Albert was a very special case in which I was actually a physical bridge for him to the outer world. I first saw Albert when he was seven years old. He had been removed from first grade at the public school because of what the school psychologist described as his bizarre and dangerous behavior. He was labeled retarded and considered unable to learn academic skills.

When Albert first walked into my office to work with me, he began speaking incoherently. At first, like most people, when I couldn't understand his words, I would say, "I don't understand you." Soon I became quite uncomfortable saying that over and over again. It didn't seem like a helpful message. Without any great insight on my part, but simply as a way of coping with the situation, I gave it up. Instead, I began responding warmly, enthusiastically, and supportively to the words I could understand. And when he babbled, I simply did not respond. As they had taught me in behavior-modification class, I simply ignored his undesirable behavior. By the end of our first session, almost all of the incoherence had dropped away, and he was communicating quite effectively with me.

After a period of time, it was recognized as important for Albert and his family that he return to a public-school classroom if at all possible. After investigating many avenues, I finally tracked down a teacher who was willing to make a place for Albert in her educably mentally retarded class. She was young, creative, imaginative, and flexible, and had a reputation for moving her students to more appropriate placements (for example, a regular classroom, or a class for the learning disabled) as soon as they were ready. The school administrator there seemed more hesitant than the teacher about accepting Albert. Knowing Albert's psychological reports, I was not surprised anyone would hesitate to invite him into his or her school. Eventually, a compromise was made; it was agreed Albert could come into her class one day each week for a month, provided I came with him to control his behavior. I agreed, since basically I viewed my role as providing a bridge for Albert from the safe place of therapy in my office to the larger world of the classroom at the public school. I recognized it would be a big step for Albert to make from one place to the other, so Albert and I decided to physically take the big step together.

When Albert became one of the students in the new classroom, I became the "teacher's assistant." As much as possible beforehand, I told Albert what to expect in class. He always knew, for example, how long I would stay there. I remained consistent and predictable and made sure there were as few surprises as possible.

The bridging had proved such a remarkable success that after the trial month, one day each week, Albert was able to attend school daily like all the other children. Meanwhile, I continued to work with him in therapy and tutoring.

I got his mother to help me, and she hired the girl next door to help Albert as a tutor. To continue the bridging, I sent notes to his mother at home with suggestions and supportive comments, and I kept in constant touch with his teacher.

To this day I cannot explain the rest of Albert's bizarre behavior reported by the school psychologist. I never experienced any of it except the babbling, but for the most part that had stopped within the hour. My guess is that because Albert was physically malformed and probably looked and sounded frightening to children, he responded to their fear with his own fear. He was afraid of them, they were afraid of him, and he became afraid of himself. They looked upon him as strange, expected him to act strangely, and he lived up to their expectations.

In contrast, because I valued Albert's presence and esteemed whatever appropriate behavior he displayed, he responded with growing self-esteem and self-confidence, and displayed more appropriate behavior. Also, in Albert's situation, I acted as a physical bridge to the school, and I continued to be that in his other relationships: between his home and school, with a girl (his tutor) in his neighborhood, with his teacher, and finally with a group of young boys in a therapy group I led.

Children, like Albert, who have especially low self-esteem will feel threatened by much of the outside world. Once you have created a safe space together—and only after this stage— you can invite them to make contact with the outside world through you. You may remain a bridge for them until they feel secure there themselves.

In bridging there are two things to remember: First, be consistent and predictable; second, let them enter the outside world at their own speed.

Self-Esteem Principle: Self-esteem thrives on success. Your bridge can provide a successful crossing.

36 ★ Let Children Use Your Strengths as Theirs

The story of Albert's move to the new school is an example of the power of this idea. My valuing of Albert, my confidence in his abilities, and even my physical presence were sources of security for him, until he was able to gain the necessary amount of self-valuing, self-confidence, and inner security.

Often enough in the first weeks and months of tutoring- therapy, what children have going for them is my belief in them. In Albert's case, both my physical presence and my emotions were there for him to use almost as if he owned them. He brought me to the school with him. For a time, I was like an extension of him. Not every child in class knew I was there for him, but Albert did.

Emotionally, too, he knew I cared about him and about his successful interaction with the class. In therapy sessions after class, we talked about how he felt toward some of the children. For example, I could help him articulate his fears about the class bully, his growing affection for the teacher, and in general a variety of feelings he was trying to get in touch with and express about different relationships. I loaned him my emotional system so he could express himself in relationships.

The way this often happened began with his asking me what I thought about his classmate John or what I felt about Miss Monica, his teacher. Did I like the food in the cafeteria? What about those noisy school buses?

I told him how I felt and then elicited his responses to the same questions, thus exploring a much fuller range of emotions. For example, I might ask: was the school bus not only noisy but frightening? Was it also fun sometimes? Did he enjoy shouting and laughing on the bus? Was it scary if the driver told them to be quiet? Did it hurt his feelings if someone didn't want to sit by him? Did some children tease or poke him? Did he want to poke them back?

In struggling to answer questions such as these, Albert slowly gained ownership of his own feelings.

I remember when Joan first came to me, her statements were confused, halting, suicidal. At seventeen, she had recently been thrown out of her own home. From what she said about our sessions, the only security she felt for a long time was my belief in her. She said it was important that I believed in her even when she didn't believe in herself. My belief in her was consistent, she said; it was always there. It was the strength she hung onto until she had worked with me long enough to believe in herself.

For example, she thought of herself as being very incompetent. Part of her fear was she would be unable to succeed at college, where she hoped to go next year. I pointed out to her when her parents had thrown her out earlier that year she had, first, gotten herself a work permit; second, a driver's license; third, a job; and fourth, a place to live. And not just another place to live but a very healthy living arrangement with a family of one of her friends, a family who really valued and liked her, and who enjoyed her presence. Had she been incompetent, she would have gone off feeling helpless and doing self-destructive things. Instead, I pointed out, she competently went about and took care of her most important needs.

Over and over I'd remind her of her achievements and successes in school, in relationships, and especially how hard she was working with me. I would say, "I don't think you're incompetent. Look what you've accomplished. I believe you're very bright and very creative."

My feelings about her and my beliefs in her were consistently positive. She counted on temporarily using my knowledge and feelings about her as her own.

Feeling she needed more of my time both physically and psychologically, she asked if she could have two sessions each week. Although my schedule was tight, and although someone on the staff suggested I was dealing with adolescent manipulation, I decided to make time for her and support what I felt was a healthy request for getting her needs met.

She had asked for something she wanted and felt she needed; and if I believed in her, I reasoned, then I acknowledged she knew what she needed. Inasmuch as I was capable, I told her, I would respond positively to that. I've always been glad I made that decision. I was willing to put my time and myself where my beliefs lay.

My esteem for her was more than rewarded by her esteem for me, and my joy at seeing her make a successful transition into college.

Self-Esteem Principle: Children's self-esteem can grow when they have access to another's perspective, love, and presence.

37 ★ Invite Children to Empathize with You

When I told Tommy about the death of my old dog Willie, he was able to empathize with me. He asked me if the death made me sad, if I had cried, did I think I'd miss the dog, and would I replace the dog? He went on to talk about his own dog. "Sometimes dogs get hit by cars," he said sadly, "and I worry mine will get hit by a car." A lot of feelings came out when he empathized with me—feelings around his own fears and caring.

You may often need to help children empathize with your feelings. To make this easier for them, focus on feelings they are likely to know themselves.

I described my daughter Julie coming home and talking about how she had been caught passing a note in class, and how embarrassed she felt. When I told her about a similar experience of embarrassment I had when I was her age, and she found herself empathizing with me, she was able to be in better touch with her own feelings and was able to talk about them more freely.

Sometimes children try to get you to tell them what they should be thinking or feeling or how they should react, rather than discovering their own unique, authentic feelings and reactions. Carried to an extreme, it would be like Harold, who at four years old used to ask me to tell him what things were and what he was feeling. He would look out the window and ask, "Is that a tree?" or he would look in the corner and ask, "Is that a telephone?" or on the wall and ask, "Is that a picture of a dog?"

Instead of answering yes or no, I would say, "Perhaps you can tell me."

I was delighted weeks later when I first heard Harold say, "I think that's a tree outside," then add, "I know that's a tree outside."

Emotionally, Harold's feelings were all lumped into one word, "funny." No matter whether Harold felt sad, angry, scared, hungry, curious, or he needed to urinate, he would say, "I feel funny." One word was all he had.

One of my tasks with Harold was to help him discriminate the variety of feelings he had and to give names to those feelings. He learned to do this most easily when he could empathize with me. If I said something was humorous and made me laugh, and showed him why, then he could understand that was one time where the word "funny" was appropriate. "The picture poster of a basket of kittens playing together," I said, "could make me feel happy. If I had a basket of kittens playing like that, I would probably feel happy."

Harold was then able to say, "If I had a basket of kittens, I would feel happy, too. I would like to have a kitten."

As Harold got in touch with a variety of feelings, acknowledged what things were, and knew he had wants, whether for a kitten or for his lunch, his sense of identity developed. He became a person who was much more known to himself.

While low self-esteemers often need encouragement to express what they feel, Harold's problems of low self-esteem were compounded because of his underdeveloped ego. He had no true sense of himself as an individual with his own feelings, needs, and an inner knowledge of the outside world. He came to me not knowing how to name things. He did not even know that things had a consistency, that is, that things stayed what you named them: a dog stayed a dog, and a tree stayed a tree.

Low self-esteemers, being much more anxious to do the "right" thing or to please others, often don't believe they have a right to their own feelings. They tend to respond primarily to avoid making anyone feel uncomfortable, so they often don't know if they are feeling angry, sad, or disappointed. They usually try to get someone else to tell them how they should feel. Persons with more healthy self-esteem will tend to accept their own feelings first before trying to integrate their experience with what others think they should feel.

There have been times when I, like almost every other parent, have denied parts of my children's emotional reality by not wanting them to express strong feelings in certain situations, or I have wanted them to express feelings contrary to the ones they were actually feeling. For example, I might want them to express gratitude rather than frustration at receiving a disappointing gift, or I might not want them to make a scene in a grocery store. I remember when a can of soup fell off a shelf and landed on Miranda's foot. Naturally, she screamed in pain. I just wanted her to be quiet, probably out of my embarrassment that people would look at me as though I had done something to hurt her. I kept saying to Miranda, "You're not hurt," while she kept insisting she was. She probably would have calmed down much sooner had I been comforting, solicitous, and soothingly respectful of her real pain rather than uselessly insisting she wasn't hurt.

In terms of being an emotional bridge for children, as it is with Joan, children need to have you express to them the areas of competence and reality you see in them. I had to repeat Joan's areas of competency over and over before she felt that competence within herself. I had to be a bridge of feeling until she was able to feel. With Miranda, however, I failed to be a bridge. I failed to acknowledge her reality of pain and allow her to express it. I'm glad her self identity was strong enough to affirm insistently what was real for her and to resist my denials to the contrary.

Adults need to acknowledge competence and feelings in children as well as affirming the children themselves. In so doing, they help children develop a healthy self-esteem that claims and values their own competence and feelings.

Self-Esteem Principle: Low self-esteem children often need encouragement to allow themselves to express what they're feeling, and sometimes they need a bridge in order to do this.

38 ★ Tell Stories about Your Life

I found that with children of low self-esteem telling stories from my childhood seemed to be the easiest way of getting them to have a more realistic perspective of themselves as not so bad, and not so different from me as a child, from my children, or from my brothers and childhood friends.

The favorite stories were always about me and my brothers, which seemed to express many of the usual experiences of sibling rivalry, and the typical, but not-so-nice, things children do to each other.

Hearing stories from my childhood and knowing me now, children could see I had grown up to become a more or less healthy, happy, normal person. I told them I got along with my brothers as an adult and though we still disagree sometimes, we no longer beat on each other physically. My stories gave the children a hopeful perspective that although things might seem quite hopeless now, they probably wouldn't stay that way.

Most children seem to enjoy hearing not only stories about my getting even with my brothers, but also stories where I simply had to live with frustration. For example, I told children how my older brothers used to take my dolls and hang them around the house—from the chandelier, from window locks, from doorknobs, from kitchen cabinets. I'd go through the house sobbing, untying my "babies," putting them back in their beds to recuperate from their hanging. But as fast as I could untie them and return them to my room, my brothers were removing them from their sick beds and hanging them again. My wails of outrage seemed only to encourage their teasing. There was no resolution to the situation. It was just a frustrating story of what happened to me.

Whenever I told this story to children with siblings, it invariably produced a lot of empathy. Sometimes children identified themselves with my brothers, and they could acknowledge how much they enjoyed teasing. Mostly, they identified with me and how much they minded being picked on or teased. They often wondered why parents didn't stop such emotionally painful behavior, and we could discuss the problems faced by parents and empathize with them because children are helped by understanding a parent's perspective also.

My younger brothers used to enjoy my telling them stories about mischief their older brothers had perpetrated. My stories bridged for them the distance of fifteen years between the two sets of brothers and showed how at one time their older brothers had been children just like them.

As I've said before, I've often told my students stories about my own children, positive as well as not so positive, especially the mistakes my children have made and the trouble they've gotten into. The students could see that I loved my children and believed in their worth, even though they had problems and got into trouble. Thus, my students could identify themselves with my children and realize that if I could love my children, then maybe it wasn't so impossible for them to be seen as lovable. They could relax in being children who were both lovable and difficult, realizing their troubles were mostly just part of being a child. Their belief in themselves and their self-esteem grew as they identified with my children and the other characters in my stories.

So tell children of your struggles, failures, successes, your emotional growth, your friendships, your rivalries, your learning. This helps them see their feelings are not theirs alone, but belong to every human being. Telling stories also introduces children to new people, new possibilities, thereby building bridges to many new places in the larger world.

Self-Esteem Principle: Children with low self-esteem often distort the world and people in it so that they become fearful and difficult to face. In times like these, children will need to use you and the people in your life as a bridge to a more realistic view of the world.

V

Fostering the Freedom
to Choose

As children enter the larger world, making choices becomes a way of asserting themselves. To be able to experience the freedom to choose predisposes children to view the world as a less threatening place, and their chances of being successful people are increased.

Developing the freedom to choose offers children a big forward step in building self-esteem. Choosing gives children a sense of having control over their lives and some sense of responsibility for themselves. It builds trust in a child's ability to make decisions and to exercise their own will and ability to discriminate. It gives them a sense of identity and self-concept as someone with alternatives. They begin to become more perceptive of possibilities, which probably leads to not feeling helpless when facing new situations or new experiences.

When children can choose for themselves the tasks to do or the skills to acquire and the means to achieve them, they will probably put more energy and motivation into their efforts, thus increasing their chances of success and their self-esteem.

39 ★ Let Children Take the Lead

I find that children who come to me for counseling often wait till almost the end of a session to state their strongest concerns and deepest fears, the issues that are really at the core of their distress. Often they had wanted to talk about these issues earlier, but they just didn't know how. As a counselor I am tempted to put words into their mouth, to name the distress or the problem before they do. To do this, however, might be to remove from them the freedom to choose when they will tell me what they want to tell me and how they want to tell it.

For adults, the challenge of this secret is to trust that children will tell you where they're at, show you what they need, and offer you what they want to share, as long as you give them an adequate chance.

They may take a roundabout way of getting to the point, and you may have to listen patiently to a lot of material they need to get out of the way in order to deal directly with their distress. I am reminded here of Sandy, who wanted to talk about her menstrual periods but didn't know how to ask her question directly, so she drew pictures of nude women on the chalkboard, which evoked questions from me that eventually led to the issue at the front of her concerns. Although it was in a roundabout way, when we did get to the point, she was very direct with her concerns; she felt relieved that I was not shocked by her, and expressed confidence that I could help her with other problems as well. Consciously or unconsciously, Sandy had more on her agenda than simply learning about how her body worked. More importantly, she was interested in building a trusting relationship with me that might help her solve other problems, and she was taking a lead in shaping that relationship.

It's very important to deal with children at their own pace in relating. This was certainly true with Hilda, who needed to be encouraged and to have doors opened for her. In order for her to feel comfortable with me and valued by me, she needed to feel that I would respect where she was in her growth. Knowing that I wouldn't push her too hard, yet would not give up on her, made her feel secure.

She also needed to know that I would follow her lead and let her choose the path we would take. Symbolically, when we walked through the playground from the nursery to my office, she might stop to push a swing and, as if we were playing a follow-the-leader game with Hilda as the leader, I would push a swing too. I did things like this to remind her that she was the leader, the director of her own growth.

Chuck was a nine-year-old boy who had been referred to our clinic by the public school as having many academic and social adjustment problems. He had thrown his lunchbox at another child and had frequent outbursts of anger during which he was apt to hit people and to throw things. It was a new school for Chuck, and he would be attending it for only one year while his parents were in the area on a year's sabbatical, after which he would be going back to his original school in Colorado. His new teacher felt she could not recommend Chuck's promotion to the next grade because of academic problems he was having. Chuck himself was terrified he would go back to his original school, be kept back a year there, and would no longer be in class with his friends. Even here in the new school there were worries. Chuck was not fitting in easily; he was not familiar with the cliques and unspoken customs of his new classroom culture. He said frankly he didn't want to be there, that he had never wanted to leave his original school and friends. His anxiety certainly affected his academic performance.

Chuck's parents and teacher asked me to tutor him in his studies and, simultaneously, work with his anxiety and social adjustment problems so he could make the move back to his Colorado school successfully. Since I had a double task, academic and therapeutic, and only four months to work with him, I chose to see Chuck in two-hour units twice a week.

I purposely didn't schedule a sequence of work for our sessions, but allowed Chuck to flow naturally from the stimulation of reading, writing, or spelling into a therapeutic dialogue with me. What evolved was a process of mutual academic and therapeutic stimulation. Sometimes a thought or a word from the class material would trigger a concern of his, and he would stop to talk about it. For example, reading a story about a house reminded him of the house he had left in Colorado, and he began wondering how well it was being taken care of by the tenants and whether they might damage the possessions he had left in his room. Thoughts of this kind revealed to him how angry and helpless he could feel about not being able to protect his possessions from so far away. He might talk about these feelings therapeutically for a while, and when he began to feel overwhelmed by them, he might suggest, "Let's get back to spelling," or "Maybe we'd better do some more schoolwork now." We'd then return to academic subjects, where he felt more secure and safe. Later he could allow himself to be triggered into talking about his feelings again. I let him take the lead in the dialectical movement from the safety of academic work to the catharsis and struggle with feelings.

The work with Chuck is an example of tutoring-therapy at its most flexible. One of this procedure's biggest assets is that it provides the security and success of academic work while dealing with strong emotional explorations. Chuck did return to his Colorado school quite successfully. His mother wrote me some months later to say they were very pleased. I was pleased, too, for Chuck had demonstrated that in taking the lead he could effectively utilize tutoring and therapy together.

Self-Esteem Principle: Children's self-esteem grows when they feel they can move freely at their own pace.

40 ★ Allow Self-Motivation to Grow

Sandy, in writing her life history, was a good example of self-motivation; she was able to enjoy the task for its own reward. Tommy's rock collecting became fascinating and gratifying to him for its own sake. It was fun for him, even when I wasn't around.

As self-motivation grows in children, you will need to rely less and less on concrete external reinforcement to keep the relationship alive. Instead, the child's own inner satisfaction will provide enough reward for pursuing the relationship. For example, Joan's journal writing that was addressed to me fostered our relationship. After a time, my approval or comments on the journal became less important than the insights she discovered for herself while writing. When in college, she would write letters to me; in the process of writing she would begin to clarify her own conflicts. She sent the letters knowing I was someone who would listen, care, and respond to her. But she was in touch with my caring and likely responses even before she mailed her letters. My responses and the security of our relationship were already inside her.

Like Joan, Wanda still liked having some external affirmations of her self-motivation. Wanda phoned me to check out her internal process by comparing it to how she thought I would respond. I realized this when after a while she said, "I knew that's just what you'd say, mom. I guess I just wanted to hear you say it." While she was obviously satisfied with her own decision about how to deal with the problem, she took the further step of calling me to reassure herself, and to reaffirm herself at the same time. She welcomed my comforting and caring, as well as my corroboration.

Albert is a good example of growth in inner motivation. His wish to do well in school proved it. He went from wanting to please me and his mother to wanting a sense of self-satisfaction (he became able to do well in school to please himself), and was finally motivated by the wish to grow in self-recognition and self-esteem. It's almost as if the esteem he got from others allowed him to move to a place where he could esteem himself. For example, in the beginning I gave Albert a piece of bubble gum each time he drew a picture as part of our tutoring session. Then came a day when he told me he really didn't need the bubble gum but wanted to draw a picture just the same. Obviously, he was enjoying the sense of satisfaction that came specifically from the act of drawing. When Albert went back into the regular classroom, I remember his teacher telling me how he was not only doing assigned tasks willingly and well, but had also begun to volunteer for some other tasks. I assumed his volunteering was motivated primarily by the sense of accomplishment he felt in doing tasks well, rather than for any particular praise or other reward he might receive from his teacher or mother. That seemed to be his teacher's understanding, too. I was happy to know Albert had continued to grow in self-esteem.

Self-Esteem Principle: As a child moves from motivation by external reinforcement to motivation from personal inner satisfaction, the sense of self grows stronger and the feeling of self-esteem increases.

41 ★ Give Rewards Out of Friendship

Maybe the term reward is more accurately called gift. Perhaps reward carries a bit of an impersonal tone, while gifting bespeaks a relationship where friends give gladly and freely to each other. I think giving out of gladness and freedom convey much more what happened with my therapy students, even though with some I followed what appeared to be a traditional behavior-modification-by-reinforcement plan. For example, while I did reward Albert with a piece of bubble gum for every picture he drew for me, I enjoyed giving it to him. I knew he liked it. If for some reason he didn't have the opportunity to draw a picture during a certain session, we both knew I would give him the bubble gum anyway. In our sessions what occurred was more like mutual gifting than giving rewards for satisfactory performance. As a gift, he'd give me a picture and a song, and I'd give him bubble gum. We were both glad for the opportunity to exchange gifts that would bring delight.

Whenever one of my students produced a story or a page of work, I would be delighted with their success. It was only natural for me to want to give them something for the joy I felt in their successes. Maybe that's a core secret of self-esteem: simply taking joy in children's successes builds self-esteem and opens the way for them to take joy in their success, too.

After a while, the successes themselves clearly produced in the children an inner satisfaction beyond whatever candy, gum, or anything else, I might give them.

I spoke of Angela who, by the way she wrapped, ribboned, and attached a gift card to the stories she wrote at home over the weekends for me, was clearly gifting me. She knew her work not only delighted me but also provided a sense of accomplishment for her. And when she gifted her friends with the cinnamon candies for their attention and for including her in their games, she showed she understood the gifting process very well.

The secret power of gifting might be stated, "You make me feel good about myself with your gifting and that makes me feel good about you." I think at times the children realize their successes were their gifts to me that made me feel good about myself. With their gifting, I esteemed myself as well as them.

My own children often asked me if I minded doing favors for them. They couldn't imagine for example, my not minding having to drive them to places they wanted to go. "It seems so inconvenient," they said. "Are you sure you don't mind?" I tried to explain that it made me feel good to do things for them.

Once my daughter Miranda was in a play. On opening night, about an hour before curtain, she discovered the skirt of her costume needed to be pressed and hemmed at least one inch higher for safety and comfort's sake, because during rehearsals she kept stepping on the hem. I said I would gladly take it home, press it, come back to school with a needle and thread, and hem the skirt, which I did. As curtain time approached, Miranda kept coming back to see how far along I was with the hemming, saying, "Are you sure you don't mind doing all this?"

I didn't know how to explain to her that I not only didn't mind, but to be sitting backstage hemming my daughter's costume was a delight to me. It made me feel needed, valuable, and important to her. I knew it would contribute to her comfort onstage and her appearance in the play. I wanted her to be as successful as possible in her role, and I wanted to enjoy her success with her. She was too caught up in her anxiety and gratitude to be able to see how much I enjoyed doing something to help her be successful. Her very success meant for me a special sense of involvement and self-esteem.

Aside from the practice of gifting, I want to emphasize that basically the idea is to promote an attitude. It is an attitude which says to children, "I want to be accepting, I want to be gifting to you in ways that will build your healthy self-esteem."

As parents, we must often walk a tightrope in trying to balance loving acceptance of our children as persons with appropriate limit-setting for them in areas of behavior. We want to give enough "rewards" to help motivate, stimulate, and encourage their personal growth, while needing often to say a firm "no" to some of their requests. We want to build in them a realistic sense of being valued and being seen as successful.

Building self-esteem in children is a delicate task; however, simple gifts and moments of loving acceptance can help in this process.

Self-Esteem Principle: Unconditional acceptance and loving rewards will help to build self-esteem in children.

42 ★ Involve Children in Choices

When tolerance levels are low among children, I found I could often develop a positive attitude toward the task when I introduced a playful note and a sense of choice regarding parts of the task.

Teddy is an example of someone I allowed to set up his own schedule for the tutoring work he did. There was little play involved in our sessions, except for picture-drawing time, but the undesirableness of the academic tasks was diluted because Teddy maintained some control and choice in doing them. The self-esteem that grew out of his sessions was owned much more easily because his success and productivity did not come through my urgings or demands. He had clearly structured, organized, and produced the work and could unequivocally own the success and personal improvements won by his own efforts.

At home, I found that when I clearly stated the tasks for which I needed children to take responsibility, it was helpful to allow them to work out the scheduling and distribution of those tasks. I helped them best when I simply kept them focused on what needed to be done and when I kept a watchful eye to see that each child's workload was fair. Julie might agree to set the table, Miranda to clear the table after dinner, and Wanda to make salad. Julie might agree to dust and empty wastebaskets every day for a week, Miranda to feed the pets and sweep the kitchen for the same period, and Wanda to load and unload the dishwasher. The following week they might redistribute these tasks.

The point was that chores themselves weren't any more desirable; however, I found the children a bit more cooperative when they had a say or a choice in the distribution of tasks. It nurtured some sense of responsibility. For example, if Julie was planning to spend the night at a friend's house, she would be expected to negotiate with her sisters for getting her task done. Usually there was a tradeoff of sorts, but I left it to them to negotiate.

I don't want to intimate that when the children had a say about chores everything was perfect. There was always a certain amount of wrangling among them, which I felt was inherent in any human situation involving choices and compromises. Also, I noticed it relieved me of a sense of having to do it all myself, or else nag them.

There were certain times in the children's lives when it was easy to make games out of tasks. For instance, when my children were quite young and loved jumping into leaf piles, it was natural to shout, "Let's rake leaves into piles," and find I had three willing volunteers looking forward to the fun of creating a mountain of leaves and playing in it. At an early age, the idea of play seemed to give every child new energy. I look back with nostalgia to those good old days.

Today, when I say, "Let's rake leaves" (that is, if I can find somebody around to hear my invitation), I am more apt to hear, "I've got too much homework," or "I'm too tired," or "Do I really have to?"

I might say, "Yes, you have to," and get a halfhearted helper who takes the first possible opportunity to abandon the task. I can't seem to turn leaf raking into a game anymore.

It might appear my children have simply grown out of playing, but I don't think that's so. I think they still love to play, but their self-concept and their sense of what is appropriate and fun has changed from the games they enjoyed at a younger age.

Self-Esteem Principle: When self-esteem gets low, keep feelings positive and play-filled. Joy and fun are universally attractive emotions and they nurture self-esteem.

43 ★ Let Trusting Be Mutual

Trust is important in building self-esteem.

When my stepdaughter Rita, aged eight, stayed with us during our first summer, it was a difficult time for her because her mother was moving their family (Rita and her older brother and sister) to another city, and Rita would be leaving many of her friends behind. She seemed generally grouchy and out of sorts with her brother and sister. I was young, and newly married with no children of my own yet, and three stepchildren to manage for the summer. At the time, I didn't know what was bothering Rita; I only knew she was easily irritated.

One afternoon she burst into tears at some little disagreement with her sister. I put my arms around her and took her into her bedroom in an effort to comfort her. Once in her bedroom, she began to cry even harder. Her brother and sister were standing at the open doorway, curious. I asked them to go and play by themselves for a while and I closed the door to make a safe and private space for Rita.

I asked her if she knew what was making her feel so badly. At first she only cried and shook her head no. I said that was okay, rubbed her back, and cuddled her. In a little while, she began to talk about her sadness and fears of leaving her old house, the friends and neighbors she knew and loved. Her fears were not so much focused on the new house as on the loss of friends from the old place. Would they forget about her, she wondered? Would she ever see them again?

I couldn't reassure her about those things, I explained, because I didn't know what the future held for her. But I could give her plenty of support and love, and a safe place to let those feelings out.

At one point I heard her brother and sister outside Rita's bedroom door; they were obviously curious about what was happening. I went to the door and asked them please to go outside and play, as Rita and I needed time just for the two of us to be alone and not be overheard. I added that probably everybody needed privacy sometime and maybe even they would, too. Then I closed the door and went back to Rita.

My statement to her brother and sister at the door seemed to be a special turning point. I think that up till then Rita had experienced an opportunity to share her feelings. But in my explaining to her brother and sister that this was not a time for listening in and in asking them to respect her privacy, she had grasped her right to deal with her strong feelings without embarrassment or being teased. I had shown respect for her needs and had asked her brother and sister to respect her needs, too, in a way they understood. It was an important moment for all three children in learning they could turn to me as someone they could trust. I became for them someone they could share their feelings with when they might be afraid to with other people, and someone they tested new feelings with.

My sense of self-esteem grew as I realized how much my stepchildren trusted me. The rights they had, which I respected, they learned to respect, too. And their sense of self-esteem grew.

I must admit I wasn't always so attuned and helpful, much as I would like to have been. Many times I missed their cues or became frustrated. But the basis for trust remained secure, and I was forgiven for my insensitive times.

The incident I remember with most regret also had to do with Rita, who had an occasional problem with bedwetting, as I discovered in doing the laundry. She was about eleven then. She wanted to spend the night at a friend's house, a friend who lived in a summer home near ours, and her father had given her permission.

When I heard about it, I was immediately concerned with what the friend's mother might say if Rita wet her bed. I feared the mother would be shocked, and I imagined how badly this would reflect upon our family. I didn't think the situation through; I just reacted. "I don't think Rita ought to spend the night," I said to Rita's father as she stood nearby, "because she sometimes still wets her bed." Rita was of course embarrassed at this revelation to her father and maintained she didn't wet her bed anymore.

Caught in my own need to prove I was right, I asserted she still wet her bed. To prove my case, I brought her stained bed sheets from the laundry hamper for everyone to see. I won my point but dreadfully wounded Rita's self-esteem and, temporarily, the trust of mutual respect. I had trampled on the sensitivities of this young child.

In retrospect, I wish I had gone to Rita instead of her father about the decision and either convinced Rita she should make other arrangements than spending the night or trusted that she could handle the situation if she did wet a bed at her friend's home. In truth, Rita's possible bedwetting was really a situation between her and her friend, and not my responsibility.

Upon reflection, I realized I had confused my own ego and my own embarrassment with hers. My need to prove I was right complicated an issue that could have been resolved in a way that built trust rather than undermined it.

Self-Esteem Principle: Children's self-esteem grows when they trust you and they ask you to trust them.

44 ★ Be Aware of Children's Subtle Messages

In encounters with children, it is wise to be on the alert to catch the signals of interest, resistance, or fear they send out.

In the situation with Rita when I had been sensitive to her needs, I noticed the subtle message that accompanied her crying. When her brother and sister were standing outside the door of her room, she gave me the clear message she didn't want them watching her cry. When they asked, "What's wrong?" she not only refused to answer, but also kept her back to them and stiffened her body. I interpreted these gestures as a need to defend herself from their curiosity.

In the discussion with Rita's father about staying overnight, I'm sure there were messages I could have noticed, not the least of which was her open denial of bedwetting, which expressed a clear need to defend her self-esteem. As she grew angrier in her denial, I could have noted she felt very much endangered. If I had looked closely at her face, I probably would have seen tautness of skin because of her tight, angry muscles. I'm sure she was showing a number of signs that indicated she felt under attack and desperately needed to defend herself.

Adults give off characteristic signs, for example, of boredom or irritation, such as finger drumming or looking at a watch. But with children, signs of boredom are often more subtle, for instance, eyes that slowly drift away or don't seem to be looking at anything.

Learning to notice signs we are losing a child's attention becomes easier with practice. Once aware of children's boredom, we can shift our approach to something that might rekindle their curiosity and involvement. Such a shift of topic or pace, sometimes with humor, calls forth our own creativity.

It is a special skill to realize when we have caught the interest of a particular child. Here, I remember Alice especially, a slim dark-haired first grader with pale complexion and big brown eyes, who often seemed to be staring off into space. Alice's parents had recently divorced, both had remarried, and Alice was being moved continually between both families. At the school, we were never sure where Alice was living—physically or psychologically. On Monday mornings especially, she might be physically present in class but mentally unresponsive.

When it came to tutoring her in reading, she wasn't present to the task. In fact, she and I often didn't seem to be in the same world. In trying to find a way Alice and I could work effectively together in reading, I realized I first had to find a way to get us involved with each other.

I'm not sure how I discovered what to do, but what I did was introduce one topic after another, meanwhile carefully watching her face and eyes for a flicker of interest that would subtly tell me I had caught her attention. Then I'd further develop that topic to the point where Alice was alert, responsive, and connected enough with the present moment to shift to the task of reading. It was the only way her energy could be made available for the tutorial work.

Sometimes my storytelling was exaggerated in order to catch Alice's interest. My motivation was to captivate her, not particularly to relay factual information. I used humor, colorful details, anything I thought might draw a nibble of interest from a six-year-old girl.

I don't know how I learned to watch for subtle messages from Alice, but it was helpful that I did. This knowledge continues to be useful to me in relationships of all kinds.

The relationship that grew between Alice and me, and her increasing ability to read developed self-esteem in both of us.

Self-Esteem Principle: When you show low self-esteemers you care enough to watch for their subtle messages, it builds their self-esteem.

45 ★ Be Prepared to Teach Liking

A primary need low self-esteemers have is to feel their own sense of self. Once they begin to like themselves, then interest in academics, relationships, and other social skills will follow.

As a tutor, the first stage of my work with children was not to teach reading or spelling, but to focus on liking. I tried to invite them to enjoy being in relationship with me, to like working together and, as with Albert and the children in the School Readiness Program, to prepare them to like school.

I felt if I prepared them to like school, they would expect to like it. Then, if I carefully helped them know what to expect, and if nothing in school was very different from what they learned to expect and experience from me, then success was most likely.

In teaching children to like school, I prepared them to feel a liking for themselves. I emphasized how they were acceptable, attractive, and valuable to me. I felt if they entered the school building believing what I said about them, they would walk in with confidence.

Once in school, if they were in an atmosphere where they felt accepted, liked, and valued, they were more likely to learn the academic and social skills being taught. They were much more apt to believe they could learn if they felt like successful, capable, and competent people. They were much more likely to respond spontaneously and positively in relationships if they had expected to be liked and valued.

So the adult's primary challenge is to prepare children to like themselves. When this happens, children tend to interpret circumstances positively (or at least realistically), rather than negatively. For example, if a teacher or neighbor says to a group of children, "You have been noisy, unruly, impolite," the positive self-esteemer will hear the complaint addressed to the entire group, accepting proportionate responsibility as a group member. In contrast low self-esteemers are much more in-clined to hear the complaint addressed to themselves alone and feel totally responsible. Children with healthier self-esteem are more likely to make a more realistic appraisal of circumstances.

Many children have a natural enthusiasm and curiosity for engaging in something new and different when it is presented as an exciting adventure. Excitement fosters liking. They are usually less excited when you stress the dangers to be avoided.

Of course, if there are real dangers to be avoided, I don't believe in minimizing them. But they can be placed in context. Like other parents, I have warned my children, for example, not to accept rides from strangers. I didn't try to terrify them by developing gory details about what might happen. Rather, I emphasized the dangers in a context of concern for their well-being and safety. I was not talking about being good children or bad. I was talking about being safe or unsafe.

Whenever possible, I found it helpful to focus on the posi-tive aspects of an experience when I wanted to prepare a child for success. To prepare children to have a clear sense of their role, their value, meaning, and importance is to help build a sense of self-confidence and self-esteem.

Self-Esteem Principle: To develop children's positive self-es-teem, their first need is to be liked, accepted and valued—especially by themselves.

VI

Dealing with
Strong Emotions

For one reason or another, many children fear expressing strong emotions such as anger, sadness, fear, or loss. To them, such emotions appear so potentially destructive they don't even allow themselves to know they're angry or sad. They're not simply afraid of looking weak and losing self-esteem when they show their feelings, though that's a part of it. What seems to them more critical is their fear of being overwhelmed by their own sadness, anger, or fear of abandonment.

Hidden and repressed feelings like these don't go away until they are dealt with. Meantime, in order to remain in control of these strong emotions, children expend tremendous amounts of emotional energy, which means they don't have as much energy available for the expression of normal feelings. When such children don't appear to be very lively or very much involved in life, it's likely certain fears and strong emotions are quietly robbing them of life on a deep level. Consequently, children need to find outlets for these emotions.

I want to say very clearly at the outset that most children have many strong feelings, and that they have a right to these feelings. The main question is how to deal with the expression of them in order that the children can keep developing their unique identity as someone valuable and keep their self-esteem growing. For this, children need to have appropriate outlets for strong, sometimes overwhelming, feelings.

I have found some ways adults can facilitate the release and healthy expression of strong feelings in children. These are expressed in the next ten principles.

46 ★ Acknowledge a Child's Right to Emotions

I have often explained to parents the importance of their child's expressions of anger in helping develop a sense of self. I stressed the importance of acknowledging the child's right to have strong feelings. It was not a matter of whether the feelings were good or bad, or right or wrong. It was not even a matter of explaining why these feelings appeared. The basic fact was the children had feelings which were a part of them. And feelings are real experiences. If you tell children they have no right to have strong feelings about something, you are denying a part of their identity.

It's often not sufficient to say to children, "Don't be afraid, it's only a nightmare." The emotional fact is after nightmares children are filled with fear.

It might be better to say, "You've had a nightmare and you're afraid. Do you want to describe it?" If the child says, "It's too scary," you might reply, "It will probably begin to be less scary if you tell me about it and we can share it together." Then hold the child and be supportive. Acknowledge the fear without increasing it. Treat strong emotions as ordinary matters people normally deal with, not deny.

When adults deny children have a legitimate right to strong feelings, it's like denying the children's sense of themselves as capable of being thinking, discriminating, evaluating, and honest persons. This is true even with young children.

I remember when one of the children had been bitten by another in the nursery school. Although the skin was not torn by the bite, the teeth marks were clearly visible, and the child was crying. The teacher was saying to the child, "You're not hurt." As the child continued to cry, the teacher kept on insisting the child was not hurt.

My concern here was that the child's sense of reality was being denied. Of course, the child wanted the teacher's attention, and in fact he might be more scared or angry about the bite than he was in actual physical pain. Instead of simply insisting, "You're not hurt," the teacher could have reflected on some of the possible feelings that were present, for example: "Maybe you're scared. Maybe you're angry. Maybe you'd like me to comfort you." Instead, the child was simply told *what he wasn't*, which left a kind of vacuum in his sense of reality. He was being told he had no right to cry. As adults, we don't have to agree with the child's view of a situation, but we can still acknowledge the child's right to his feelings.

I've often heard people, young and old, say, "If the other person was right, then you had no right to be angry," as if one's rights to feelings could be turned on and off according to whether someone is morally just or unjust.

I am reminded of another incident in the nursery school, when Rachel got angry because Cindy spilled paint on her dress. Rachel claimed she'd done it on purpose, while Cindy maintained it was an accident. Rachel grew angrier and angrier, screaming that Cindy had done it on purpose. In trying to calm her, the teacher assured Rachel that Cindy hadn't intended to spill paint on her, but that "it was an accident."

All Rachel could sobbingly reply was, "She ruined my dress. And she did it on purpose because my dress is ruined."

Moreover, as we found out between sobs, Rachel was also scared she would be scolded by her mother for getting her dress messed up. "My mother told me be sure not to get this dress dirty because we're going out after school."

To this, the teacher responded comfortingly, "Cindy didn't

do it on purpose, and you didn't get your dress messed up on purpose."

Rachel asked, "Do you think my mother will know I didn't do it on purpose?"

The teacher promised Rachel she would explain the whole thing to her mother, and assure her that Rachel hadn't been careless or disobedient.

It's important to note here that both Rachel and Cindy were caught in a similar emotional bind: The frustration of not being able to prove they hadn't done something on purpose. In addition, Rachel got angry at Cindy because she knew her mother would get angry at her; she was passing her mother's anger on, ahead of time, to the person to whom she believed it really belonged.

The subtle implication in the incident, which is supported by the teacher's first comments, was that since the paint spilling hadn't been done intentionally, Rachel had no right to her anger. Yet Rachel knew she felt very angry. Eventually the teacher realized she needed to affirm Rachel's right to be angry about her stained dress, because that in itself was very upsetting and something about which the child had every right to be angry. Furthermore, she explained, Rachel could be angry even though Cindy didn't do the spilling intentionally. Indeed, too, Rachel's mother had a right to feel angry about the stained dress without having to assert that either Rachel or Cindy intentionally caused it.

Rachel's self-esteem could be protected by assuring her she had a right to her angry feelings. Cindy's self-esteem could be preserved, too. That she had caused the stain didn't have to be denied, but she did not have to accept or be made to feel guilty that she had done it intentionally.

In the end, both children came through the experience with a better understanding of how parents could become angry at something like a soiled dress without labeling their children "bad." And the girls could see that parents act fairly without having to suppress anger or other strong feelings. In this way, the children would continue to esteem their parents.

Self-Esteem Principle: When children's strong feelings are accepted, they feel respected and valued, and can allow their strong feelings to be a part of their reality. Growth in self-esteem is connected with children's acceptance of their right to have strong feelings.

47 ★ Provide Outlets for Strong Feelings

Many children are probably afraid to express strong feelings because they have been told not to: Don't be afraid; don't be hurt; don't be sad; don't cry; don't be angry.

In my work with children the command I'm most familiar with is, "Don't be angry." Somehow it is suggested to children that being angry is like being bad.

Children with low self-esteem are particularly hesitant to show feelings for which they can be criticized or for which they might feel rejected by others.

Some children have rejected so much the part of themselves that could get angry that their anger is never allowed to be expressed. In some extreme cases, children no longer even feel their own anger or know they can be angry. In Hilda, her fear of being angry had almost paralyzed her.

Once I took the lead in exploring an outlet for Hilda's anger that worked. Before our sessions, I used to treat Hilda to a bottle of soda. Together we'd walk downstairs to the soda machine, I'd give her the coins, then I'd lift her up to reach the coin slot. When the can of soda came out, we'd take it upstairs to my office and enjoy it.

One day the machine took our money but didn't give us any soda. I tried pushing all the handles and buttons. The machine still refused to deliver our soda; it wouldn't give us back our money, and I had no more change. In frustration, I kicked the machine and said, "Darn old soda machine!"

I knew Hilda had trouble showing any strong feelings, particularly anger, so I suggested Hilda could kick or hit the machine if she wanted to.

She took one small kick at it and then began to cry in fear. I picked her up and showed her she hadn't hurt the soda machine. In fact, as I was well aware, it was impervious to our assault. I assured Hilda it was okay to be angry at the soda machine; it was okay even to hit it and let the machine know we were angry because it had kept our money and not given us soda. I assured her it was very different from hitting a person.

After my explanation, I put her down, took her by the hand, and started to go upstairs. To my surprise, Hilda turned, gave the machine a slap, and stuck out her tongue at it. Then we left.

I'm not sure how this event worked its change in her, but she became more open with her feelings after that.

For example, in the next few sessions she made a number of requests to play ball with me. She would throw the ball as hard as she could. Next she asked if she could shoot the rubber dart gun at the puppet in my hand. She would giggle with delight as I made loud groaning sounds on behalf of the puppet. She was apparently discovering she could explore some violent expressions of feelings, like hitting, throwing, kicking, and shooting, in ways that were acceptable and non-damaging.

She also discovered she could pull the head off one of the dolls and I could put it back on again. Her insight was that sometimes damage could be repaired; it didn't always have to be final and irreversible. It must have been a satisfying discovery for Hilda, because I had to put that doll's head back on many times in the next few weeks.

My music box had inside it a Jack-in-the-box, who would jump out unexpectedly. (One never knew how many turns of the handle would make Jack jump out.) Hilda had always been startled by Jack before this. Now she was learning to enjoy the feeling of surprise and began to giggle whenever Jack jumped out of the box at her.

She was discovering that many feelings and behaviors she had considered fearful or unacceptable could be explored in the creative and dramatic play that happened in my office. As she expanded the realm of feelings she could tolerate and enjoy, her sense of trusting herself grew, and with it her self-esteem. She acted more alive, more energized, and more involved in the world. And she seemed to be having a lot of fun doing it. All of this newly discovered vitality created in her a more alive and positive sense of self.

Self-Esteem Principle: When children's strong feelings can be set free and their repertoire of feelings expanded, they feel a growing sense of freedom, and their self-esteem grows.

48 ★ Allow Strong Feelings Time to Cool Off

When children come to you in a state of embarrassment or anxiety, don't confront them with their feelings immediately. It's better to spend time together in a gentle way until they regain their sense of self. Only when a climate of loving and caring has been clearly established are they usually ready to begin facing their strong emotions.

Sometimes embarrassment doesn't really need to be talked about directly because children deal with and work through it in their own internal way. In this case, all you have to do is provide the caring and supportive atmosphere in which that can happen.

As I mentioned before, Tommy, either because of his inability to express himself adequately in the classroom or because of his innate shyness and discomfort at being the center of attention when asked to respond in class, would sometimes come to a tutoring-therapy session distraught, distracted, out of sorts, and having lost his sense of self.

At times like these, Tommy would ask if we could do something outside. He wanted to be in a place where he felt comfortable and could enjoy a special sense of harmony with nature. There he would take the time to work through his strong feelings and regain his sense of self.

If the weather was bad, he might deal with his anxiety by asking if we could begin our session with picture drawing. In the creative expression of himself, he could regain the equilibrium that allowed him to approach the rest of our tutoring time with energy and confidence.

Sometimes, after spending time outside or drawing pictures, Tommy would talk about whatever had upset or embarrassed him. He'd explain the situation in which it had occurred, ask me what I thought, tell me how mad he had been or what he'd like to do to the people who made him angry or hurt his feelings. At other times he seemed to handle the strong feelings internally, while he searched for rocks outside or drew pictures in the serenity of the tutoring room.

He knew he was free to talk about his strong feelings, but he also knew he didn't have to. And he knew I would respect his privacy. Early on we had established his right to talk to me or not about what was bothering him. Once when we had come inside from gathering rocks and Tommy immediately went to his books to begin work, I asked solicitously if something had been bothering him and, if so, did he want to talk about it.

Tommy confronted me very gently but very directly, "Do I have to talk about it?"

I said, "No, Tommy. You never have to talk about anything you don't want to talk about with me. I understand. Sometimes I feel that way, too."

So I learned not to ask Tommy, and Tommy learned that it

was okay not to tell me if he didn't want to, but I would be a receptive listener if he needed one.

Children will often suggest a way you can help them deal with strong feelings. I can remember sitting on the steps next to Miranda with my arm around her while she gazed off gloomily into space. I knew something was bothering her, said so, and told her I was sorry she wasn't happy. A few minutes later she asked me if I would take her on my lap and rock her as I used to when she was a little girl. As I held her, we talked about how she used to like being rocked, and she shared some of the memories she had of it. We never did talk about what had been bothering her that day. Growing peaceful with the physical closeness and memories of happy times seemed to be enough.

There have been many times when, particularly as a parent, I have been impatient about wanting to know what was bothering my children. And when they told me they didn't want to talk about it, I kept asking, pushing, wanting to know. My insistence sometimes caused more distress than comfort, and at certain times we ended up, my daughter and I, in a tug-of-war over the situation, instead of joining sides and facing the problem together.

In demanding to have their feelings aired with me, I created an additional problem with my daughters: I was not respecting their right to their own privacy. And when I didn't esteem their right to choose their own way of dealing with their strong emotions, it must have appeared I didn't esteem them either.

Generous as my wish was to help them face whatever caused their embarrassment, I first had to esteem their right to choose for themselves how they wanted to deal with their feelings and what, if anything, they wanted to share with me.

Self-Esteem Principle: To maintain self-esteem in times of strong feelings, adults need to help children build patterns of response to strong feelings which increase the probability of a successful outcome.

49 ★ Connect Yourself with Their Strong Emotions

The simplest and most natural way to connect with children in emotionally-laden situations is to share a story of some similar embarrassment or anxiety you went through.

As I have said many times already, I used to connect with strong feelings in my students and clients by telling stories of my children or of my own childhood. It was important to my students to have some sense of how I or my children had struggled through embarrassment or anxiety, and some idea of how my story might apply to them. Not least among the messages was that if other children had survived their embarrassments, so could they.

For example, many children dread the kinds of school games and activities where teams get chosen: two team leaders, usually the best in the class, get to choose their team members one at a time. Wanda had often talked about how awful it felt to be standing there while sides were being chosen and she knew nobody wanted her because she wasn't very good, whether it was in soccer, softball, or spelling.

Wanda always had trouble spelling. She often spelled words phonetically, rather than according to the dictionary. In spelling contests in class, she was often nearly the last, if not the last, to be chosen. To Wanda it seemed that the class leaders were secretly talking about her as they chose teams, saying, "You take her, I don't want her," as she stood there embarrassedly waiting to see to which team she would belong.

Since spelling contests still seem to be a perennial part of school experience and since many of the students I worked with in learning disabilities had major problems with spelling, they could usually identify themselves with Wanda's embarrassment and be able then to talk about their own.

They often asked me if Wanda ever got to be a good speller. I'd say truthfully, "No, but she did get better, and she uses a dictionary a lot when she writes." Sometimes this would lead to an opportunity to teach them how to use a dictionary.

Wanda also had a very great fear of getting hurt physically. The fear of being hit by a ball kept her from becoming a very good player in sports. Again, many learning-disabled children with whom I worked had perceptual problems and could not accurately judge where a ball would come; they shared Wanda's fear of getting hit and usually had problems with not being good players. So Wanda's embarrassment in not being chosen for teams and in thinking of herself as an undesirable and poor player was something they could identify with and then talk about.

Like Wanda, I could admit remembering what it felt like to be left out on teams, and how my anxiety and embarrassment grew as I waited and waited to see myself not being chosen and feeling undesirable.

The point here is not that the children and I became comrades in mutual misery, but that we talked about an emotionally-laden problem we shared and could see it was probably shared by many people. From that perspective, our problem and the emotions it churned up in us didn't seem quite so awesome and overwhelming.

They could identify my children's situation as being similar to theirs. They could also identify with the respect and valuing I still felt toward my daughters, and so not feel overly diminished themselves. Somehow, I could continue to respect and esteem them even if they didn't appear very competent.

Another realization I hoped would occur to them was maybe now they could acknowledge their own ability to empathize with other people and begin to see how helpful empathy was in building relationships and a sense of mutual self-esteem.

Self-Esteem Principle: Children with low self-esteem are constantly afraid they will lose even more self-esteem in embarrassing situations. This belief may be counterbalanced by the perspective of time and the example of other children's experiences.

50 ★ Help Children Get Emotional Distance

When children are likely to be overwhelmed by strong feelings, it is often useful to find ways to help children find a bit of emotional distance from the events. Here are four ways I have found helpful:

First, make up a story showing how the situation could be worse and, when possible, do it in a way that might be humorous. Laughter is always helpful. The time Julie came home after the teacher had intercepted her note, we used this idea by talking about some other messages she might have written in the note. We decided one message might have been the teacher had bad breath and brown teeth. Though such a message might be calamitous, it was also funny and gave Julie a moment of laughter and some emotional distance. We went on to improvise other hypothetical and humorous messages. As they grew more outrageous and funny, what had been put in the original note no longer seemed quite so awful. The laughter not only helped put things in perspective, but also relieved some of her anxiety-energy.

Second, since sometimes some of the details of their story are too painful for them to deal with directly, ask children to make up a similar story about what happened to somebody else. I have a therapist friend Victoria who has a rather remarkable technique in this respect; it helps her clients deal with strong feelings such as helplessness, inadequacy, being a poor friend, frustrations, and so on. She tells the client's story in the third person, as if it were a fairy tale. If she were talking to Julie she might begin, "Once upon a time there was a little girl named Julie who liked to have fun and make her friends laugh. She also liked to talk, and when she couldn't talk to her friends, she sometimes sent notes . . ." Victoria would go on to tell the rest of Julie's story from this integrative perspective. She would emphasize Julie's positive qualities, like enjoying life and liking friends, so the embarrassing experience was seen as merely one event in a much bigger picture. Victoria's fairy tales were invariably of someone who was lovable and capable.

Third, ask children who are caught up in strong feelings to make up a new ending to their story, an ending they would have preferred. In order to achieve the necessary emotional distance, it is usually not sufficient to settle for, "I'd just rather it hadn't happened at all," but to take the facts and create a new final act. As in Julie's case, the fact was that a note was passed by her and it was intercepted by the teacher. I invited Julie to take it from there. She was able to come up with, "Then the teacher dropped the note in the wastebasket," or "Then one of my friends grabbed the note and swallowed it." Psychologically, by playing with alternative outcomes, Julie was gaining some distance and processing some of her anxiety by talking about it. The event probably no longer felt like the most important thing that ever happened in the world.

Fourth, ask children to act out their story to help drain off anxiety and embarrassment. Wanda used to receive numerous embarrassing and self-esteem-wounding comments from her third-grade teacher, whom I will call Mrs. Meany. When Wanda came home depressed and upset at having been focused upon and embarrassed in class, her stories were often talked about at the dinner table. In fact, our dinners often ended with Wanda doing an impromptu dramatization of Mrs. Meany. Wanda would stick out her stomach and waddle across the floor as a short, fat Mrs. Meany and shake a crooked finger at all of us around the dining-room table and shriek, "Nowww, children . . ." in a caricature of her raspy-voiced teacher. As we all laughed together at the "Lectures of Mrs. Meany" and saw her as this ridiculous character of Wanda's dramas, some of Wanda's anger, anxiety, and embarrassment drained off in a healthy, entertaining way. With our laughter, applause, and obvious delight in her characterization, Wanda was able to re-establish her sense of self-esteem.

Mrs. Meany continued to have power to embarrass Wanda, but Wanda had found a way to keep that embarrassment from becoming a festering, lingering wound. It got drained and healed regularly.

I haven't any way of knowing if there is a connection here, but Wanda has gone on to become very gifted in acting and storytelling. It's possible Mrs. Meany originally triggered Wanda's career.

Each of these four methods of inviting children to manipulate the events of their story allows them to take the story in their own hands and control it to some degree. The ability to step back and play with their story allows children to reestablish a sense of ownership of their life. They become aware of their own power and not just someone else's power.

Self-Esteem Principle: When children are able to distance themselves from their own embarrassment or anxiety, it is a sign strong feelings haven't consumed them and self-esteem can be renewed.

51 ★ Help Relieve Stress with Something Physical

When children are being put into an unavoidable stress situation, for example, being given a test, meeting new people, or facing a challenge, some physical outlets to drain off excess anxiety are helpful. These might include something to touch, hold, squeeze, stroke, rub, bend—something that allows them to release anxiety through physical activity.

With Sandy, who had to be tested periodically by an outside

evaluator regarding her progress in remedial academic work through tutoring, I was very conscious how her test-taking anxiety got in the way of her successful performance.

I noticed how anxious Sandy was when she and I went through a mock spelling test in preparation for her classroom spelling test. When I saw how she played with and often broke a pencil in her anxiety, I tried giving her a hunk of clay to mold, a rubber ball to squeeze, or a stuffed animal to hug. The object she manipulated allowed her to release anxiety through her hands as she worked verbally at the spelling test.

Tommy was the first of my tutoring students scheduled to be tested who talked freely about how he wished it could be me who would be the tester and how nervous he was at the thought of being tested.

On the day I was going to do a mock testing with Tommy as a preparation for the actual test, I brought my own pet dog to the clinic, because I knew how much Tommy liked dogs. Tommy held Willie on his lap and petted him as he worked verbally at the testing with me. The harder his mind worked, the harder his hand petted. Willie seemed to enjoy it all. The anxiety that flowed out through Tommy's petting freed his mind to function more adequately. It also put a very special and pleasurable aspect into the testing situation.

With both Tommy and Sandy, the testing preparations had gone so well they were psychologically relaxed and ready for success in the actual test situation. And both did remarkably well. Being relaxed had made a significant difference. With less anxiety and a more realistic esteem for their own ability, they performed accordingly.

That I also cared enough about Sandy's and Tommy's anxiety to find ways to help them deal with it made them feel supported and secure. They knew definitely that I was on their side and that I would do everything I could to help them be as successful as possible. I was cheering for them, and they knew it.

In the end, this test did not have the adversary quality about it for Sandy and Tommy as tests usually did. (Sometimes tests feel as if teachers are trying to find out what you *don't* know so they can be critical of you.) Tommy and Sandy knew my intent was not to criticize but support, that I was not their adversary but more like their teammate or coach.

Willie's friendliness and appeal overflowed too, so the total environment felt more friendly and appealing to Tommy. All of this was designed to build for him a place where he felt safe and valuable, esteemed by me (as well as the dog), and more in touch with his own peacefulness and growing self-esteem.

Self-Esteem Principle: As a friend, you can be foresightful enough to provide ways of releasing anxiety in children since children with low self-esteem might never think of it or know how to do it for themselves.

52 ★ Show You Can Accept Even the Undesirable

Most children with low self-esteem keep trying hard to prove they are unlovable and incompetent.

A number of children I worked with had been with other tutors previously. When that tutoring hadn't proved successful, the children felt like failures—hopeless, discarded. When their parents contracted for them to work with me, it felt like they were now going to have to face those feelings of failure one more time with a new tutor. They were prepared to feel hopeless. They certainly didn't accept their own possibility of success.

Again and again, I found no one had ever explained to the children the dynamics of what went on in their lives, whether it was their inability to read, to speak clearly, to concentrate, to socially interact. It was Tommy who told me adults always just said, "You don't pay attention to what I say."

So I asked Tommy a few questions about his daily life. I

learned that at home a great deal of Tommy's time was spent in the presence of Spanish-speaking maids. Generally, these women talked to each other but not to Tommy, because he didn't understand Spanish. So he tuned them out. And it became a habit with him to tune out people nearby who weren't talking directly to him or capturing his interest. When I learned from Tommy about the situation at home and asked him if he thought it had anything to do with his not paying attention to people, he said yes. The foreign-speaking women at home didn't explain all of Tommy's learning problems, but thinking about it did help him see some of the habits he picked up weren't because he was a bad boy. They had happened naturally and understandably, as a response to daily experiences.

It took Sandy quite a while before she told me she thought she was retarded. Evidently it was a very embarrassing admission for her. I was surprised at her revelation and asked her why she thought she was retarded. She explained how compared to other children it was much harder for her to read and spell. I told her I thought she was really a bright child but had a learning disability—what people call dyslexia—which was quite different from being retarded.

No one had ever explained to Sandy what went on in her brain, what her learning disabilities were, and why they were there. So I talked to Sandy about her own learning problems.

Generally, if I talk to children about dyslexia or learning disabilities, I avoid the term brain damage because it sounds scary to them. Sandy, I found out, had overheard her mother saying she had brain damage, and Sandy thought that meant she was retarded. I asked her if she knew what had caused the brain damage.

"Yes, I do," she said. "When I was two years old I fell down two flights of stairs. I was even unconscious for a long time. The doctors didn't think I would live."

I acknowledged to Sandy her symptoms indicated brain damage, "But brain damage has nothing to do with your being bright." I explained how her fall had probably caused damage to some of her nerves and cells, which meant she would need to find special ways to learn. Indeed, I assured her, we had been doing just that, and to help her learn in new ways was my job.

"Your fall did not take away your intelligence," I assured her, "it just made it harder for you to learn in the usual classroom ways. In fact, you must be very intelligent to have learned to read and comprehend as well as you do, since reading words in proper sequence is very difficult for you."

From time to time we would talk about the way her mind worked so she could be reassured she wasn't retarded. Anytime I could, I would point out some of the real gifts she had. I told her I thought she was quite gifted and explained to her what it meant to be gifted.

I am always distressed when I come across a situation where children have not been told about themselves in clear, affirmative ways, but left to draw their own frightening conclusions or be misnamed by other children. Children with low self-esteem are particularly likely to fixate on the worst possible conclusions about themselves and live year after year in a hopeless state.

Self-Esteem Principle: If I can see and understand the undesirable in children and still accept them, then they come a bit closer to understanding and accepting themselves.

53 ★ Help Children by Telling Stories

The point of telling stories about the failure and misfortune of people dear to you, such as your children, your spouse, or your friends, is that they have failed or gotten into trouble—yet you still like them and accept them as they are.

I mention storytelling again because it is such an important technique, especially in dealing with powerful emotions. Children can identify themselves with characters in a story as they would when watching a play or reading a novel. The hope is by identifying with a character, children will be able to deal with some difficult experience or strong feelings of their own.

Most children I've worked with, and my own children, too, have asked me at one time or another if I ever failed a test, been rejected by a friend, been called names, received an *F* on a report card, got sent home from school, got caught doing something bad, and so on.

I've told students my daughters have asked, "Will you still love me if I get an *F?*" I am able to assure them I still love them even when they experience failure.

It's normal for children who fail to wonder if they are alone in this experience or if there are others to whom this same misfortune has happened. I don't ever hesitate to describe the kinds of misfortunes I experienced or witnessed as a schoolgirl.

In first grade, a little girl named Marie was too shy to raise her hand when she needed to go to the bathroom. Lots of us were shy, since these were the first days of school. Luckily, I never felt the sudden urge to go to the bathroom at an unscheduled time as Marie did. She wasn't a very noticeable child—she was short, thin, and quiet. I hadn't noticed her at all until she suddenly started to cry loudly. The whole class turned to look at her. She blushed harder as she became aware of all eyes focused on her and cried more intensely. The teacher walked toward her and exclaimed, "Oh, my goodness!" as she looked at the floor and realized Marie had wet her pants. A huge puddle had formed under her and was now beginning to make its way along a row of seats. The class was sent outside for an extra recess, for which we were grateful, and Marie's needs got dealt with.

I think a number of us in class identified with Marie's embarrassment and were relieved it hadn't happened to us. We really didn't view Marie as having done something bad. We went all through the primary grades with her, and it didn't seem to have scarred her or her relationships at all. Although it was surely a dreadful moment in her life and a strong memory for some of us classmates for a number of years, it did not keep her from being an accepted, valued, successful member of the class.

The children to whom I've told this story have no trouble identifying with Marie's embarrassment, and it often touches off memories for them of friends and classmates with similar embarrassments. They are then able to see misfortunes and failures fall into a moment of time in a longer perspective. Stories like Marie's can help children get a balanced perspective, even in the midst of strong emotions.

Storytelling allows children to empathize and sympathize with another person like them in a similar situation. If they can have caring and concerned feelings (sympathy) plus understanding, acceptance, and support (empathy) for that other person, then maybe they can feel some of that sympathy and empathy for themselves. They can also realize that others like me or their classmates can also have caring and supportive feelings for them.

Furthermore, if they can also view what happened to someone in a story as something humorous, they might be able to view their own situation with a bit of humor, or at least a bit of tolerance. If they can say, "What happened to her wasn't such a big deal," then maybe they can see how their misfortune isn't such a big deal either, at least in the long run.

When I was the character in the misfortune story, as it sometimes happened, the children could be in touch with their current esteeming of me and see I had not only survived a similar misfortune but had gone on to become someone they respected and wanted to befriend.

Self-Esteem Principle: Storytelling allows children to identify with a failure situation and experience it without direct anxiety. It also allows them to get a more realistic perspective.

54 ★ Encourage Children to Talk to Other Adults

It is sometimes helpful to redirect children with high emotions to a third person. Children's self-esteem can be strongly threatened when they must deal directly with the people with whom they are highly emotionally involved.

Parents are often unable to view their own children objectively. This realization became clear to me when I taught first grade and had my daughter Miranda as a student. As a teacher, I saw how well she was doing in the context of a whole class instead of just as my child. My appreciation of her became much more realistic than it had ever been, and my evaluation of her grew more objective. I also became amazed at how much more appreciative and relaxed I was with her at home now.

In contrast, when Wanda had been in first grade (and I saw her only at home), I was more anxious and concerned about the mistakes she might make, for example, during a reading lesson at home. In fact, I would often focus on her mistakes rather than on how well she was reading.

When listening to Miranda read in class, I could see her mistakes, but I learned rather to focus on how well she was reading in relation to other children.

I have come to appreciate the value of a new perspective in strong emotional situations. A class of high-school seniors had requested that before they graduated and lost their strong mutual support system, they wanted to air certain misunderstandings and problems that existed between them and their parents. In particular, several of the students were interested in going on to college, but they wanted to take a year off first. In contrast, some parents adamantly insisted their children should go directly to college. At least one set of parents had said if their son didn't go directly to college, they would never help him finance the rest of his education. Many strong feelings were being expressed by students and parents, and some

firmly held values were colliding. Some very unhappy stale-
mates had recently occurred concerning student values, prior-
ities, everything from the way they dressed, handled family
responsibility, and performed academic tasks, to the way they
spent money, viewed working, planned for the future, and saw
their place in the world. Values, identity, and independence
issues of late adolescence permeated the struggles of these students with their parents.

The plan we worked out was students and parents all came
to our home on Thursday evenings for six weeks. At the students' suggestion, parents and students were to be mixed together into two groups, but no student would be in the group
containing his or her parents. In this way, all parents had to
relate to children not their own, and all children had to relate
to parents not their own. One group met in my family room,
the other in the living room, each group out of earshot of the
other.

Over the first month, both parents and students, each at
their own pace, developed openness and listening skills. They
learned to communicate well across a generation because they
as parents didn't have their own emotions tied to their own
children directly confronting them, and likewise for the children.

On the fifth evening, parents were put into groups with their
own children to talk about some of the issues they had been
discussing in the earlier weeks.

During the sixth session, everyone came together in one
group. By this final meeting, we had moved from a place of
listening to someone else's parent or child (practicing the skills
of clarifying and listening nondefensively) to using those skills
listening to one's own parents or children. It proved to be an
evening of healthy communication in a large group. The six
weeks of meetings had evolved into a celebration of mutual
support.

Many of the parents and students remarked how much easier

it had been to listen to someone else than to the person they were related to. Their own self-esteem was not as vulnerable hearing someone else's parent or child, therefore they did not have to be as defensive. The emotional climate was less volatile. They were able to hear and respect the value system of another person which was different from their value system and still feel esteem and respect for that person, as long as that other person wasn't someone in whom they had invested much strong feeling. In that context, they could think more openly, express themselves more freely, see more alternatives, not feel as locked into a position, not be so defensive, and not have so much at stake emotionally.

Self-Esteem Principle: Children's self-esteem can be strongly threatened if they must deal with adults with whom they are directly involved in emotional problems and value conflicts.

55 ★ Help Ground Frightened Children with Facts

When children are caught up in strong feelings or imminent fears, they need to be connected with positive potentials in the future. Such a connection is best made when you focus on simple concrete facts about the near future.

When I was the person who handled emergency service at the clinic on Fridays and encountered someone making suicidal statements either on the phone or in person, I would immediately begin relating to them in a personal, caring way. Then I would make an appointment with them for a therapy session on Monday and say I was looking forward to seeing them then.

Basically, what I did was give the suicidal person an obligation to stay alive and make a visit to the clinic in the near future. Since the patient and I had initiated a relationship during the first contact, he or she could feel an obligation to our newly begun relationship. And the expectation (to meet on

Monday) that became a part of their reality could help carry them over the crisis of the suicidal feelings.

A story about Teddy belongs here. His grandfather had died the year before, so a number of nights each week Teddy stayed overnight at his grandmother's house because she had a bad heart. He felt he was responsible for whatever happened to her on those nights.

One morning Teddy burst into my office telling me his grandmother had almost died the day before. She had been working in her garden and he was helping her. Suddenly, she felt a lot of pain in her chest and had difficulty breathing. She asked Teddy to go into the house and get her heart medicine. Teddy looked for the medicine in every place he could think of. Nowhere could he find her nitroglycerine tablets. He was so terrified, he said, his heart hurt and he wanted to throw up. Finally, he ran back to his grandmother, sure that she was dying and that it was his fault, since he couldn't find her medicine.

He described to me how he had stood helplessly near his grandmother repeating, "Grandma, I love you! Grandma, I love you!" He was afraid because he couldn't find the medicine she would think he didn't love her.

Teddy said he didn't mind the responsibility for his grandmother, but on a deeper level he felt his own helplessness. He needed to find a perspective to help him deal with his fears of not being able to live up to this responsibility. The reality was he was not able *always* to be there and be responsible for his grandmother. He had to go to school, for one thing. He needed to realize his sleeping over in her home did not guarantee his grandmother would not die in her sleep without his knowing it, that even if he were awake and could find her medicine, the medicine might not always make the difference. I wanted, in short, to help Teddy realize he did not have the power to keep his grandmother alive, even if he did feel the responsibility. Nevertheless, this responsibility continued to weigh on him and, in fact, Teddy was known to be suicidal because of it. He was given to saying to me he wished he could die and go to heaven with his father and grandfather, and if anything happened to his grandmother he would kill himself.

At the end of the school year, when I knew I wouldn't be seeing Teddy until the fall, I handed him a toy as a token of my caring and appreciation of the time we'd had together. Teddy said he had a gift for me, too, but he'd forgotten to bring it.

"But I'll bring it next year," he added.

"Fine," I said. I realized it was his way of saying, "If you want your gift, you'd better be here next year."

When I said I was looking forward to seeing him then, he said, "I'll be here unless my grandmother dies. Then I'll kill myself."

I responded, "You can't kill yourself, Teddy, because you owe me a present."

He smiled a great big smile and said, "Oh yeah, that's right."

He had been promising to kill himself for so long he needed an excuse not to do so. He was obviously relieved to have an out: bringing my present to school next term.

Self-Esteem Principle: When children are put in touch with actual concrete things they can do, the overwhelming fear of responsibility can be removed or put into perspective.

VII

Inviting the Affirming Spirit

This book is about inviting into the world the miracle of growth, the unique spark of the divine spirit, which every child contains. It is within this spark that there lives all the hidden potential that waits to be realized over a lifetime: The ability to learn, to relate, to grow, to create, to love and be loved, to feel alive and powerful in the world, to be able to trust and feel compassion, to be playful and curious, to enjoy the new as well as the familiar, to forgive mistakes, to take risks, to give affection and receive it, to want to touch and be touched deeply, to laugh at the humanness of things, and to reach beyond oneself. In all things, the affirming spirit strives to bring forth one's own unique self.

The following principles are designed to help you facilitate a child's potential in ways that tend to foster self-esteem positively and affirmatively.

56 ★ Help Children Be Positive about Themselves

Children with low self-esteem generally find it difficult to see and name the positive specialness in themselves. Instead they tend to sprinkle their conversations with negative self-image comments.

David, who was eleven, would have been tall for his age if he stood up straight. His large brown eyes gave the impression he was trying to hide from the world. Not only did he have trouble reading, but if you talked with him for very long, it sounded as though he had trouble with everything in his life. During our first session, I focused on our getting to know each other. Since it was winter, I suggested the weather was good for ice skating, mentioned I liked to skate, and wondered if he did.

"Yes," he replied, but then put himself down by saying, "I'm not very good at it." It didn't sound like the best topic for getting involved, so I decided to try another.

"My favorite time of year is really summer," I said, "when people can go swimming. Do you like to swim?"

"I guess so," David said, but immediately negated himself with, "I don't know how very well."

I decided on a different tack altogether. "Who's your best friend?" I asked smilingly.

"Mark," he replied, "but Mark moved away, and none of the other boys at school really like me."

This series of replies, each one carrying a self-put-down, are fairly typical of a low self-esteemer's way of thinking about himself.

In working with David to build in success, I was especially conscious to point out things he did well. I emphasized he didn't have to do things exceptionally well from the beginning, only to learn at his own pace.

I suspected it was possible that some of his eagerness to put himself down was to protect himself from being criticized. People couldn't criticize him because he beat them to it by criticizing himself. I also felt his self-expectations were unrealistically high: he demanded of himself that he ice skate very well; he couldn't simply enjoy the fact he could ice skate.

I found it important with David to find reading material about which he could be excited; he needed the excitement to give him an extra push to counterbalance his natural fear of failure; for example, to create excitement, I devised a game for looking up spelling words in the dictionary and learning their meaning. Searching for words turned into a treasure hunt, which led to finding a hidden piece of bubble gum. The adventure of tracking down the bubble gum, my delight in his success, and capturing his reward all helped David to focus on success rather than failure.

After this, David began to perform better in the classroom, and his attitude toward himself began to change subtly. One of the ways I could tell was that in conversation he no longer added those negative disclaimers about his abilities. He could simply affirm himself by saying, "I like to skate," or "I like to swim," or "I've got a friend Mark."

I noticed that whenever my daughter Wanda received a good grade on a paper or a high mark on her report card, she'd be apt to disparage her accomplishment. While some children feel they need an excuse for getting low grades, Wanda felt she needed an excuse for getting high ones. Wanda found ways to deny her own accomplishment, put herself down, and keep herself from really valuing herself as a bright student. To me it indicated an area where self-esteem was lacking.

When I confronted her by saying, for example, "Why don't you acknowledge you did very well?" or "Why don't you admit you worked very hard and handed in a very good paper?" she consistently resisted admitting she did anything well. She could admit she worked hard, but couldn't allow herself to say she was capable of doing some things extraordinarily well.

I pointed out this habit of hers and teased her gently about it, and in a good-humored way generally tried to get her to see how she denied herself. Maybe with enough support from me, she'll get more comfortable esteeming her academic self as I do. I look forward to the day when I will hear Wanda excited and pleased with her good marks, no longer needing to explain away some of the good feelings.

Self-Esteem Principle: When low-self-esteem children stop making disparaging comments about themselves, it's a probable sign of growing self-esteem.

57 ★ Tell Children How Well They Are Growing

Children growing in self-esteem manifest many changes: they look more grown-up, more in control of themselves, more poised and self-confident. Generally, they seem more outgoing, even walk straighter with their heads up instead of looking at the floor. Relationships with peers often improve markedly, and so does their school work. Telling children the signs of growth you observe in them facilitates the self-esteem process.

That's what I did with David. I constantly pointed out to him how he was succeeding, what he was learning, how much he had learned since we began working together. I often showed him how many pages we had completed in his class workbook. On my desk I kept a growing looseleaf notebook of his stories and drawings, which, I reminded him, represented his hard work and talent. In another notebook, I kept his spelling words—on each page was a word, divided up into syllables with a short definition, just as in the dictionary—so he could watch his own progress as the stack of pages grew. I talked to him about the many signs of improvement of which I was aware. I encouraged him to join me in discussing and explaining their significance. I told him he was in the process of learning "mastery." He really liked that word.

I was impressed with David's mastery, the effort he put into his own work, his growing enthusiasm, his increasing ease of talking self-affirmatively with me. And I told him so, again and again.

Originally, David came to our sessions speaking with a slight lisp, which must have been exaggerated by his sense of anxiety. The lisp became less noticeable as his ability to express himself verbally grew and as he allowed himself to acknowledge my valuing of him.

In an earlier chapter, I wrote at length of Sandy, how her self-confidence grew and her self-image changed to that of a competent, lovable, valued person, as she learned to express herself through dialogue with me and through creative writing.

Back in the classroom, the teachers of both these children described them as having "bloomed." The children looked different, the teachers said, they stood erect, held their heads up confidently, no longer had the hiding look in their eyes, seemed more mature and fleshed-out as persons. Instead of being "not there," the children now seemed to have substance, presence, spirit. I noticed this as well as the teachers. And their classmates noticed it too. With the other students in the class, they seemed more confident yet relaxed, more welcoming and welcomed, more interactive and alive in their responses.

Sandy, who had always been a loner and often came to see me during her lunch hour rather than be totally by herself, first made a friend with whom she played jacks outside my door. Soon she began conversing with other students I tutored and developed a friendship with them. In her class, she not only began to participate more and agreed to help write the class play, but even dared to accept one of the speaking roles in the play, which she proudly invited me to see, a risk she never would have dared take when I first knew her.

It's been suggested something more was happening to these children than learning how to spell and developing their egos. The development I refer to as a sense of self is really a spiritual growth. What happens when children are blooming is their spiritual sides are growing. There is a transformation in these children, and whether you want to call it blooming or something else, whatever name you give to describe the force at work, it has to do with the development of the inner self, the spirit. And it shows externally in their urge to relate, a growing gracefulness, a zest for life. I loved the children, but I didn't change them. They transformed themselves. The growth happened inside them. In these pages I have tried to examine and share how I facilitated it.

As for this other quality, this force that works at the deepest level, I don't know how to name it except to say I brought with me a belief in it, and passed this belief onto the children. It was Joan who said I believed in her when she didn't yet believe in herself. I brought to children my belief in their ability. They were valuable to me and I believed in their valuableness, they were lovable to me and I believed in their lovableness, they were capable to me and I believed in their capabilities. I wanted my belief in them to stay with them, no matter where they were and no matter what the circumstances. I wanted to stay spiritually present to them and to be a spiritual support to them always. Somehow that inner connection between us happened and was understood by the children.

To touch the life of another human being is to have your life touched. And to touch the soul or influence the spiritual growth of another human being is to feel that touch upon your own soul and your own spiritual growth.

Self-Esteem Principle: Self-esteem in children manifests itself by transforming them in physical, emotional, social, and spiritual ways.

58 ★ Take Delight in Finding Hidden Wellsprings

In thinking about the spiritual growth that often happens in children, I am reminded of a sense I sometimes have of having touched a *hidden wellspring* in a child. That was the way I described the experience the first time it happened with David. It seems to be related to inner growth, but not as permanent.

Usually when I worked with David, he struggled with concepts and tasks, trying to express himself, to find the right words and articulate them properly. At these times I would feel myself struggling along with him; his sense of effort was very real, almost palpable.

But there were other times, very special times, when his mind would simply open for him: concepts seemed effortlessly easy, tasks flowed, he spoke freely with an assurance and clarity of articulation beyond my usual experience of him. At these times, he seemed to be operating from a different level, where many of his normal hindrances and blocks simply didn't exist. It was like looking at a clear spring of sparkling water that bubbled up—fresh, bright, clear, pure—from some hidden source deep within him.

I never knew the secret of how to tap that hidden wellspring in him or in any other child. I only knew how to recognize it, to delight in it, and to enjoy the beauty of the moment when it happened. I'm not sure parents or teachers were ever aware of these moments. David never talked about them, nor did any of the other children whom I noticed having them.

With Albert, for example, there were wellspring moments, like the time when he first put together the doll house exactly as it was pictured on the box cover. He had gone about the task with sureness, brightness, directness, freedom, self-confidence. Supposedly retarded, he was assembling something I wouldn't have been able to do in the short time he took. Diagnosed as having a short attention span and an inability to concentrate, he did the task with a surety and concentration which I would be challenged to match. I couldn't explain it. But I watched it happen.

In order to notice wellsprings in children, I think adults have to work very sensitively and intensely with them. Wellsprings may be detected in the subtle changes taking place in a child's ability, performance, creative expression, body movements, and even posture.

For me, the gift in the wellspring experience is in knowing what it could be like for the child, knowing the potential really there deep inside.

It's important to remember these wellspring experiences are only moments. If either you or the child expect things always to flow so well, you have very unrealistic expectations. On the other side of the coin, these miraculous moments remind you there is something to hope for, more potential waiting to be realized.

Self-esteem is enhanced in children when they know they have such a capacity. Because they have experienced it, if only for a moment, they can know this potential is also a part of who they really are.

Self-Esteem Principle: When children's self-esteem is growing, the hidden springs inside them tend to appear.

59 ★ Be Ready to Have Your Concern Tested

Often the test of your concern comes in the form of behavior children know would be socially unacceptable. So be ready for it, expect it, and recognize it as a situation with growth potential when it happens. It is important for children to know you would not reject them for their words or actions, and that your primary concern is for their needs and protection.

Sandy was a good example of this approach. At various times, she tested my acceptance of her, especially before she was able to trust me with questions and information about herself that were very frightening or emotional. When she drew pictures of a naked female body, I avoided judging the behavior as good or bad, looked for the message in her action, and showed my concern by helping to bring her questions about sexual development to the surface and finding helpful, clarifying answers for them. At an earlier time, she had asked me if I would still like her if she used a certain four-letter word. I assured her I would still like her no matter what words she used.

It was important to explain that I could love and accept her as a person, without liking her behavior or agreeing with her. We then went on to talk about the possible consequences of using such words freely around other people. She realized other people's reactions might not be as accepting and concerned as mine. As her trust in me grew, she began telling me about her other behaviors, such as the fire setting. We had by this time set the tone of our relationship and agreed that I would be honest and objective, keeping her interest in the forefront of my mind when I listened to her. Her question, "Will you still like me if . . .?" had been an important signal that a primary question on her mind was, "Would people love me or reject me if they knew about my worst behaviors?" She herself knew she needed help in dealing with them, but first had to find out where she stood with me.

Every child I worked with tested me. In working with Albert I recognized he needed to learn something all children need to learn: to play games according to the rules and to be able to tolerate losing. Since I was preparing Albert for reentry into school, both academically and psychologically, I worked with games challenging enough to stimulate creativity and intellectual growth. What this also stimulated in Albert was what I like to call creative cheating. While in another child I might utilize some aspect of creative cheating to build upon, I felt Albert needed to learn I would stick to my word. My word was that we played each game according to its rules. If he didn't understand a rule, he was free to ask for clarification at any time. If he broke a rule, I would explain the rule correctly once more. However, if he broke the rule a second time, I would end the game. It was hard for Albert not to break the rules, since he found it very difficult to lose any game. It was a very special day for both Albert and me when we finished a game that he lost and he was able to say, "I liked playing the game. But I like it better when I win." With a hug, I told him it was certainly much more fun to win, but I was proud that he was able to play by the rules, even when he knew he was losing. I told him he was a good sport. However, this did not end Albert's need to test me on the limits I set with him.

When parents don't set clear limits and guidelines, children may feel that their parents really don't care about them. My point is that limits are still important, even if they are broken many times. Children will keep testing the limits you set, but remember that what they are ultimately testing is if you really care enough about them and their safety, nutrition, sleep, and other needs.

Limits and the reasons for them need to be talked about with children so they can understand how your loving and caring is operating in the limit setting. It is also helpful when children can be involved in decisions about the rules and limits that concern them. Of course, parents are ultimately responsible in a family and carry the final authority, but it's helpful for the self-esteem of the children and fosters the self-esteem of the parents when limits and rules are worked out in an atmosphere of mutual trust and concern.

Children need to know they're loved. I can't stress this enough. They also need to understand the difference between being loved and their behavior being acceptable or unacceptable. Children need to feel your loving constantly enough to tolerate the times when their behavior meets with disapproval in order for them to test and develop their own identity and values. Even when you may not approve of their behavior or agree with their values, you still need to show that you love them and accept them as persons.

Self-Esteem Principle: Children with low self-esteem usually find it easier to accept themselves if you show you are concerned about them and can accept them, especially when their behavior seems unaccceptable.

60 ★ Respect the Specialness of Names

When relating to children, don't presume to call them a certain name; instead ask them what they choose to be called. Also, give them a choice of what to call you. To build self-esteem in them, let them name themselves, name you, and describe the relationship between you as they see it. Basically, this concept has to do with inviting a certain amount of control and responsibility in children for how a relationship is to function.

When as a tutor I met a child for the first time, I would often say something like, "I understand your name is Charles. What would you like to be called?" He might choose "Charles," but he might also choose, "Chuck," "Charlie," "Butch," or some other nickname he preferred. From then on I would address him by the name he requested.

I would tell the children my name was Mrs. Pat Berne and ask them what they wanted to call me. Some seemed more comfortable addressing me as Mrs. Berne throughout our sessions, others began with Mrs. Berne but switched to Pat, still others started calling me Pat from the beginning. I'm not sure that one name or the other could be used to measure a child's sense of relaxation or relatedness to me. The factor I focused on was that naming me was a choice I gave them. It underscored my concern. It said, "Whatever name would be most comfortable to you will be most comfortable to me—whether we're talking about your name or mine."

Children regard their names as a part of who they are. Their own name is very special to them; it has almost a magical quality; it is very much connected with their inner spirit. I can remember teasing one of my little brothers by insisting his name was Frank rather than John. I remember his frustration and outrage when I denied his true name; to him it seemed to be a threat to his very identity.

Absentmindedly, I sometimes call one of my daughters by her sister's name. It is generally frustrating to them, as if I had not valued their uniqueness enough to look and see or listen to the daughter with whom I was interacting. Such a mistake had an effect on their perception of how I valued or devalued them and what they had to say.

The use of nicknames meant only for family use or nicknames conferred by special friends is a gift in a relationship. For someone outside the family or close circle of friendship to use one of these special nicknames without the child's permission is often viewed as an intrusion into a very private space.

The point in all this is that children's names are a very special part of their identity and strongly influence their self-esteem. Naming is a gift given mutually in a caring relationship. Giving children the privilege of naming you is a gift you may want to offer them in an atmosphere of welcome and esteem for the relationship.

Self-Esteem Principle: Children's self-esteem grows when they feel a sense of control and respect in how they are known by people they like and admire.

61 ★ Make Encounters Appealing through Novelty

Introduce novelty in activity, in tools, in words, in tasks, in colors, and shapes. Anything that looks new and fun-filled is apt to be attractive to children and motivate their interests. Whenever children feel their own inner attraction to something, they are motivated to know it, explore it, spend time with it, and value it. While self-motivation provides a drive for success, success helps build self-esteem. That was my basic principle throughout my work as a teacher and therapist, and to the degree that I was conscious of it, I tried to put it into operation in all my relationships with children, including my three daughters and my three stepchildren.

In teaching and tutoring, I introduced novelty at the very beginning of each new relationship by bringing in fascinating objects, such as prisms, kaleidoscopes, crickets, and pets, in order to attract children into relating to me. That was the first step. Then I used novel tools and techniques that seemed like toys and games (and sometimes were) to make the learning of academic skills seem like fun. For example, as I mentioned before, with several children I taught reading and sequencing using the Sears catalogue. I taught reading, writing, and comprehension by utilizing jokes, poems, riddles, limericks, magic tricks, and scientific experiments. I taught reading and composition through the children's own storytelling and books they wrote themselves. I taught measurement using crickets and friends. Kerry taught counting by having children jump up and down stairs and by noisily pushing chairs from one side of the room to the other.

Self-Esteem Principle: Children's self-esteem grows when interaction is attractive and appealing and has a sense of freshness or novelty geared to their special and unique interests.

62 ★ Use Humor in Building Relationships

Relationship encounters are usually more inviting if children expect they're going to be fun, and maybe even funny. Using humor effectively requires paying special attention to the relationship. In order to be humorous, you can't merely superficially attend to a child, you must be very present to the nuances of the interaction. Humor is often based on a special awareness or sensitivity regarding the child.

I've always found it easier to present a difficult task, whether to a student or to one of my own children, if I could find some way we could laugh together about it. For example, when I was trying to get my daughter to clean up her room and complaining about the closet stuffed with all the debris that had originally been spread throughout the room, she and I were both able to relax a little because I seasoned my dismay at the closet by adding some humorous fantasies concerning it. Here were a few of the statements I used: "I opened the door and thought I was going to be buried by an avalanche," and "Did you get your friends to help you stuff that closet?" and "I thought one of the dogs might be in there, and I would not have been surprised to find you had stuffed your sisters in there as well," and "Actually, you win a prize for getting so much stuff into your closet. The prize, however, is a fun-filled evening of closet cleaning." I closed with something like, "And I want you to remove not only the dog, the cat, the mice, and whatever else should not be in a closet, but also the things that belong in dresser drawers, your desk, your bookshelf, and in your sisters' rooms—from which you can smuggle them back again some other time."

My statements may have come across as a bit sarcastic (if I remember rightly, I was accused of being sarcastic), but I think there were a few smiles for both of us in the exchange of dialogue. And I think the instructions to clean up may have been a little easier to hear because of my attempts at humor.

In tutoring children, I found that the use of humor could often be made a part of the work. For example, I remember once teaching spelling where the child was to write the new word on the chalkboard as I wove the same word into an ongoing humorous tale. In order for me to continue the story, the child would have to spell correctly the next word on the list.

Working with Hilda, I relied on things that would amuse her in order to draw out her interactions with me. Her first vocalizations, a response to humor, were done through the puppets who snored loudly, coughed, sneezed, and groaned, all of this in the context of a story I was weaving with the puppets as main characters in a comic drama.

Jokes and riddles proved to be a humorous way of facilitating learning. Sandy's limericks and poems were often considered by her to be funny, especially when they were "naughty."

Laughter can be a healing force. When I've helped a child deal with an embarrassing situation by exaggerating it until it could be laughed at, or by casting it in some laughable drama, I'm sure the wound of embarrassment had healing salve put on it.

To be able to laugh at one's mistakes and human frailties has always been healthy, helpful, and healing for wounded self-esteem.

Self-esteem is also involved with seeing oneself as an entertaining person, someone people enjoy being with. It makes you feel good about yourself for having made others laugh and smile. Your self-esteem grows when you can bestow the gift of humor. I often remark to children: "What a gift your sense of humor is! How helpful it will be in your life!"

I recall a counselor friend saying that she thought what helped us survive in our counseling work was that we had developed a warped sense of humor, one that kept us constantly looking at ourselves and life with a certain amount of amusement, no matter how serious or emotionally heavy things became. I propose that people in general, but especially those who have to work with children, would do well to develop such a warped sense of humor and to look at life through glasses tinted with amusement.

Self-Esteem Principle: Humor can be a great antidote for low self-esteem, especially when children want to get out of their low state quickly.

63 ★ Touch Often Speaks Louder Than Words

When I'm working with a child, I try to move sensitively to the emotional place where the child might willingly accept being physically touched by me. I might touch children on the back, shoulders, or top of the head long before I allow myself to give them a spontaneous hug, even though I might feel like it.

Children often have a very strong sense of their body as their private property to protect. While as adults we might be used to giving a social kiss or an affectionate hug to all members of an extended family or to friends, children reserve this privilege only for very special people. Sometimes parents suggest children kiss everyone in the room good-night, at an extended family gathering for example, and find themselves with a child who doesn't want to comply with their wishes; it's probably because they don't yet feel the closeness to all of these people that a kiss instinctively symbolizes.

On the other hand, parents are sometimes just as concerned when they find one of their children has developed a crush on an adult and wants to sit by them, cuddle up to them, and monopolize their attention and time.

In both situations, parents need to be sensitive to what is appropriate for the child as well as the child's feelings, and act accordingly. In the case of a crush, the parent may want to say something to the child that both acknowledges the warm attraction and also sets some limits to expressing it.

I often use touching as a way of conveying caring feelings. I was especially aware of using touch when I worked with young children. For example, when I was proud of Albert's work, I put a hand on his shoulder and told him how proud I was of his working hard. Many times I reached over to touch his arm as a reassurance I was still with him as he struggled at a task.

When Albert and I walked down the hall together on the first day at his new school, I didn't presume to hold his hand for fear he might be embarrassed if other children saw this. However, he chose to slip his hand in mine as we walked for the reassurance and comfort he seemed to need. I held his hand gladly but lightly, so he could take it back easily if he felt he needed to.

Sometimes touch is the most appropriate response in a situation with a child. I can remember my own children waking from a nightmare, or having some frightening experience during the day. I would hold them and rock them, or rub their backs with rhythmic, calming strokes. Though I might be saying words meant to reassure or calm them, I think it was really the rhythm of my touch, added to the soothing tone of my voice, that calmed them down and brought their emotions back under control.

I can remember seeing Mrs. Chilton holding a very upset child whose mother had recently died. As soon as the child began the emotional outburst, Mrs. Chilton took the child on her lap and wrapped her arms around him. She was holding him so firmly that he couldn't thrash or kick. She explained to me that it was sometimes necessary to physically restrain and contain a child's emotional expression when a powerful feeling overwhelmed them and they couldn't control it by themselves. That would be a time when touch, though forceful and restraining, was appropriate to the child's strong emotions gone out of control. It was indeed a touch that both she and the child understood and trusted.

Touching can help enhance a child's sense of being valued and esteemed. Your sincerity toward children's needs helps them accept their own needs and value their own feelings. They learn to esteem themselves through the esteem and caring they feel in your touch.

Self-Esteem Principle: Children's self-esteem grows in proportion to the depth of trust reached in a relationship. Physical contact can be a most fundamental expression of trust.

Afterword

Throughout this book I've been talking about successful ways to build self-esteem in children.

Mrs. Chilton's premise in educating children had been: success builds on success. Taking her premise one step further, I asserted: success helps build self-esteem.

I have presented many principles and techniques for assuring success but, as I mentioned before, success alone doesn't guarantee the growth of self-esteem. There is an important relational component that makes all the difference in whether children perceive you as skillfully manipulating their success or caringly facilitating it. It is your loving attitude in the relationship that says to a child: "I'm your friend not your adversary. I'm on your side and we face this task together." Ultimately, both success and self-esteem will blossom healthily in children when these are planted in the loving, caring relationships you establish with them.

I had a letter today from one of my daughters expressing an important insight about self-esteem. "This may sound awful," she wrote, "but it's *nice* to have people worry about you. It makes you feel like you're worth more than you thought." Her final sentence sums up a primary need of a low self-esteemer:

something that "makes you feel like you're worth more than you thought." Children with low self-esteem need to feel, see, and hear—so that they can finally *know* internally—that they are worth more than they thought and that this worth is alive, not only in them, but in a loving relationship with you.

It is quite a challenge to love and support children in self-esteem producing ways. Please don't be discouraged by what you haven't done. Rather, I invite you to be encouraged and take heart in what can still be done. Trust the affirming spirit, examine where you are, and begin building a more loving world with children from there.